An Experience
of Norway

Patrick Davis

AN EXPERIENCE
OF NORWAY

David & Charles
Newton Abbot London
North Pomfret (VT) Vancouver

For Mary who came with me

0 7153 6644 0

© Patrick Davis 1974

Set in 11 on 13pt Aldine Bembo and printed in
Great Britain by Latimer Trend & Company Ltd Plymouth
for David & Charles (Holdings) Limited
South Devon House Newton Abbot Devon

Published in the United States of America
by David & Charles Inc North Pomfret Vermont 05053 USA

Published in Canada by Douglas David & Charles Limited
3645 McKechnie Drive West Vancouver BC

Contents

Acknowledgements

Dan Sinclair, Tor Neumann, Hilda Davis and my wife read and usefully criticised parts or all of drafts of this book. None can be blamed for the final job, for they have not seen it. I am most grateful for their help.

For the maps I am indebted to Eunice Wilson and Janet R. Baker. Every writer on travel will appreciate how good it is to have willing professional collaboration in this vital matter.

For producing the final typescript I have to thank Jean Ali.

From time to time I have quoted from other writers on Norway. All travel books build upon the work of earlier writers. This book is no exception. May I here express gratitude to the authors listed in the bibliography. Their works have always been useful, and many have given me great pleasure.

Illustrations

7

Plates 2, 5, 6, 7, 8, 9, 10, 11, 12, 16, 17, 19, 21, 25, 29, and 30 are copyright of the author. Grateful acknowledgement for permission to reproduce the other photographs is made to the following to whom the copyright belongs: Export Council of Norway for plates 23, 26, 27; The Mansell Collection, for plate 28; Popperfoto, for plate 4; Royal Norwegian Embassy, for plates 1, 3, 13, 18, 22, 24; Tromsø Museum, for plate 32; Universitetet Museum, Trondheim, for plate 31; and Widerøe's Flyveselskap and Aerofilms, for plates 14, 15, 20

MAPS

For ease of reference the maps have been placed at the end of the book. Almost every place mentioned in the text is on a map, though a few have had to be left out for lack of space. Conversely, no attempt has been made to put in roads, places etc not mentioned in the text, though a few such will be found. Because Norway is a long country, we have had to make the map of North Norway to a smaller scale than those of central and southern Norway.

Preface

This is the story of a six-week, 4,000-mile journey. Within the space available I have tried to convey information—on places, history, things to see, things to do—but I have kept to the thread of the actual journey, for I think that only in this way is it possible to recreate the sense of discovery that every journey should give, and which is a great part of the pleasure of travelling. My wife and I returned to Norway the following year, 1973, for four weeks, when most of a first draft of this narrative was written. It should be clear from the text when I describe something that was seen on that second journey.

The reader will find no information on hotels, for only once on either trip did we enter a hotel. There will be no help in locating the best restaurants and the food to eat in them, for we could not afford such places. Our journey was done in a motorcaravan, the covered wagon of our time. We carried our beds with us, could go wherever roads and tracks and ferries would take us; where they stopped we could walk, and often did. For the most part we ate what could be cooked on a couple of gaz burners and a grill. This is not a book for the sophisticated; neither is it one for the mountaineer and long-distance walker. It is intended for the mass of people somewhere in between, who like to travel and who have to do so cheaply. Incidentally, while on these trips and while preparing for them, no official knew that I had a book in mind. The help we received was spontaneous and would have been given to any other traveller.

Norway is a rewarding country to explore. It is beautiful every-

where. Obviously the traveller does not come to it for the great
man-made masterpieces of European civilisation—though there is
more of value than one might expect. But for scenery, for endlessly
varied and continuous beauty of nature, of mountain, fjord, sea,
river, waterfall, moorland and forest, there can surely be no country
its equal.

In part Norway's attraction is the absence of man. It is not true,
as one official booklet states, that 'even during the peak season you
can drive for miles without seeing a car'. It is true that off the main
through routes you can drive for miles and see few cars. By walking
only a little distance you can escape these. For this reason it really
is worth trying to organise a journey through Norway on your
own, or with a small group, for when you travel with a coach
party you carry your crowd with you and cannot accept Norway's
gift of solitude. But go by coach if there is no other way.

On the whole Norway is a country that rewards movement,
whether on foot, by car, bus or train. The weather can be superb,
and you can get as brown sunbathing among the skerries of the
south coast as anywhere in Europe. But you cannot rely on doing
so. Norwegian weather, though much warmer in summer than
might be expected, is not predictable. Be prepared for rain—which
brings its own beauty to the mountain scene—make full use of the
fine days, and plan a holiday that moves you about a little, if only
into the next valley.

This is not a comprehensive guidebook. Although we motored
4,000 miles, there were some areas we had to miss: North Norway
beyond Narvik, for example, and the south-west around Stavanger.
But you will, I hope, get from this book a taste of the country,
and a taste for it. You will learn a little of its history, its geography
and its civilisation. You will perhaps be encouraged to see for yourself and to find out more.

1 Bergen

The approach to Bergen from the sea must be among the most beautiful harbour approaches in Europe. To emerge on deck in the morning was like a rebirth. There was a fresh breeze, there were high white clouds, and ahead a distant barrier of mountains was joined to the ship by a glittering sun-path.

In time the mountains rise and the nearest land resolves into a line of low islets, grey rock with saucers of grass and an occasional shrub, no trees, a few huts each with a landing stage. There seems no gap in this skerry-guard until the boat is close. Then quite suddenly she slips through into a wide fjord, then a narrow one, twisting down ribbons of blue water corralled by rock. Finally, across open water, there is Bergen strung athwart the lower slopes of Mount Fløyen, unassailably safe, one would suppose, behind a double screen of islands and peninsulas.

Off and on there have been human beings on this west coast for at least 8,000 years. Sailing in as we did, cushioned by the comforts of a modern liner, it is easy to forget that until very recent times wind and human muscle powered all ships. It was from the country-side around Bergen, before ever the city was founded, that many of the Vikings set out for Iceland in a great burst of emigration towards the end of the ninth century.

In the Icelandic Sagas little is made of the voyage between Norway and Iceland, though even today it is a small adventure. 'When they were ready to sail they put out to sea and had a good passage. They landed at Bergen, and Thorid wasted no time in asking whether the king was in residence . . .' (*Hrafnkel's Saga and other stories*, 95). But sailing into Bergen near the tail-end of our twentieth century one is bound to recall those tough traders of the viking age, who roved these channels between these same capes, hills and hidden reefs, accompanied, it is certain, by the same scavenging gulls.

Bergen is now in size of population (113,000) the third city of Norway, after Oslo (482,000) and Trondheim (128,000).* For many centuries it was the first. Perhaps it was never the spiritual capital, but it was the largest, richest and most cultured town from at least the early thirteenth century until 1840. Not until the mid-nineteenth century did Oslo grow to be a true capital,† and not before 1967 did Trondheim's population outstrip that of Bergen.

Until the completion of the railway between Oslo and Bergen in 1909, and between Oslo and Trondheim, in 1880 on the Røros line, communications between the cities were slow, difficult, sometimes dangerous, and mostly by sea. For much of Bergen's history it was a quicker sail to Scotland than to Oslo, and more profitable. Bergen has always looked outward, has always been cut off from the rest of the country by its mountain hinterland.

Bergen is the capital of western Norway, the mountainous fjord province of Vestlandet. It was founded as a trading centre in about 1070 by Olav the Peaceful (who also founded Stavanger, and the Cathedral of Nidaros at Trondheim, see page 58), but grew to European importance from about 1350 when the Hansa merchants from Lübeck in Germany, already long settled in Bergen, fully organised their 'factory' and gained control of the city's external trade. The evidence for this meets the visitor soon after disembarking (if he has sailed in), for the docks are close to the city centre. Along Vågen, the northern edge of the inner harbour, and near its eastern end, lies Bryggen ('the Wharf'), where in the last of a series of much photographed, gabled houses is the Hanseatic Museum (*plate 1*). The museum house was built in 1704 after the fire of 1702 had destroyed the medieval buildings.

* Population statistics for Norwegian towns are a puzzle. They vary widely according to what boundary is taken. The figures given here are from *Mini-Facts about Norway* 1972.

† Oslo was called Christiania or Kristiania from 1624 until 1925, but to avoid confusion it will be called Oslo here, whatever the period.

One soon learns that every Norwegian town has at intervals been
gutted by fire—the price for building in wood. Few old buildings
survive, and few archives. Much of central Bergen was burned out
again in 1916. The past of a whole nation has been destroyed with
appalling regularity. Only in this century, with the twin inventions
of concrete and archaeology, has a process of resurrection and
preservation begun. The Norwegians are still finding out who they
are.

The Hanseatic Museum is interesting both as a building and for its
contents. The interior is dim and cool and smells of wood. It is
furnished as a Hansa merchant's house of the sixteenth century. In
the house with the master and his secretary lived and worked a
bundle of apprentices; their cramped box beds, within view of the
secretary's bed, are a feature of the upper rooms. There was no
heating. Light came from lamps fuelled by cod-liver oil. The
apprentices, it is said, were not allowed to fraternise with the locals,
and certainly could not marry them. Their love-life must perforce
have been illicit, for though at the height of Hansa power the factory
held 3,000 German merchants, journeymen and apprentices, there
were few German women. This compact colony of male strangers,
armed and pugnacious, was not subject to Norwegian law.

The chief reason for Hansa interest in Bergen hangs from the
ceilings of some rooms in the museum—dried cod. The Hanseatic
League, centred on Lübeck, eventually comprised an alliance of over
a dozen powerful merchant cities, and in return for loan finance
demanded monopolies that gradually gave them entire control of
the external trade of the Baltic and Scandinavia, reducing northern
Europe almost to colonial status. Bergen was chosen because its
location was the best from which to monopolise the trade in dried
and salted cod from western and north Norway. Dried fish was
important to Catholic Europe, with its embargo on the eating of
meat on Fridays. Subsidiary interests of the Hansa were furs, skins,
whale fat, cod-liver oil and walrus ivory.

The Hansa could be a rough and brutal crew—on one occasion
they killed sixty people in Bergen, including a bishop and some

priests. Whenever the Norwegians rebelled against these excesses, the Hansa cut off supplies of corn, which they alone imported. It was not until 1559 that their power declined sufficiently for the Danes, who had controlled Norway since 1380, to challenge them. Under the guns of the fortress the Germans were ordered to take up Norwegian citizenship. Some left, some complied. Bergen was again open to trade with many nations and it flourished: in the seventeenth century its trade was greater than that of Copenhagen. But the Hansa bequeathed a lasting impression on Bergen, as did the French on New Orleans and the Moors on Madrid. More than mere buildings survive.

It is worth ferreting between and behind these old wooden houses on Bryggen. Though the buildings have been renewed, the ground plan is very old, dating from medieval times, perhaps earlier, for there are records of a settlement of sea houses here, with gables facing the sea, even before the foundation of the town. The houses stretch back several hundred feet—a splendid large-scale model of them can be seen in the Historical Museum—and there are at least two narrow passages down the length of them from the street. Along these there are overhanging eaves, roofed gantries with chains for raising goods, wooden balconies and arcades, all romantically streaked with sunlight and deep shade. According to the *Bergen Guide* handed out free by the information office (a large circular kiosk in the centre of Torgalmenning), Bryggen is 'a growing centre for arts and crafts, where painters, weavers and craftsmen have their workshops'.

Every sizeable town seems to have an information centre. They are worth visiting. The English brochures vary, but some are remarkably informative and usually give the opening times (often limited) of museums, galleries, historic buildings and other targets. And if self-catering, as we were, it is vital to know when the shops close early—on Saturday afternoons in Bergen.

When travelling, reactions to a place can depend on the weather;

they may be soured by persistent rain or lifted by sunshine. Bergen has a terrible reputation for rain (72 inches a year of protracted drizzle, according to one writer). Indeed all along the seaward edge of the fjord country, and again on the higher slopes of the western plateaux, the statistics on rainfall are daunting. Here air warmed by the Gulf Stream meets air cooled by the mountains, ice fields and glaciers. Yet on both our visits to Bergen we had hot sun.

If you are equally lucky, take the funicular up Mount Fløyen (1,050ft). It is necessary to look down on a city to get a proper idea of the relation of its various parts to each other, and of its setting in the countryside. Maps do not have the same impact. And most Norwegian cities are obligingly close to mountains. From Mount Fløyen there are splendid views over Bergen's harbours, lakes, islands and fjords.

At the top station you will find a restaurant and a choice of pretty paths, with pine scents, lush grass and mosses, heather and flowers, lakes, ants and red squirrels. The funicular operates until midnight; it would be beautiful to go up after dark, if there is some dark. For us in late July the stars never quite made it. From the southern suburbs there is a cable car up Mount Ulriken (2,000ft) which provides even wider views and more walking.

Of the regular tourist sights, I would not give the sixteenth-century Rosenkrantz Tower a high place unless you are entirely unfamiliar with the medieval fortified buildings of northern Europe. Masons from Scotland carried out the original work and it has that dour look of a Border castle. The Tower was destroyed when a German ammunition ship exploded in April 1944 while moored at the quay a few yards away, and what the visitor sees now is mostly restoration. There is a good view from the parapet, where you can also touch the roof tiles that are of extraordinary size and thickness. Beyond the Tower the Haakonshallen, a thirteenth-century royal hall, was destroyed by the same explosion and has also been restored.

There are a lot of museums in Bergen. Which to visit if your time be limited must depend on your interests. The Historical Museum is up by the university (founded 1946) at Sydneshaugen, of which it is a department. The museum is beautifully laid out, is not bewilderingly large, and there is a short guidebook in English. You should certainly look at the rooms labelled 'the Bergen collection' on the first floor. The model of the Hanseatic League's trade-quarter at Bryggen has been mentioned. There are other models of Bergen at different dates, numerous topographical paintings of the city, and a fine collection of local furniture and fittings. On the second floor examples of folk art, arranged by districts, are on display.

It was room 4 on the first floor that surprised us. Set high on the walls, like the prows of so many medieval galleons at anchor in some ancient harbour, there is a row of post-Reformation pulpits. It was for us the first intimation of that wealth of painted carving that is such a feature of Norwegian art, and to see it massed in close array like this was a revelation.

The Reformation was imposed on Norway by the Danes during the middle decades of the sixteenth century. There seems to have been little hostility to the Catholic Church, and little spontaneous support for the teachings of Luther among the scattered population, who were naturally conservative, naturally suspicious of foreign ideas. Not until the next century did such ideas take root. Today the Norwegian Church is a Lutheran Established Church and claims 96 per cent of the population. Whether such a number 'believes' in any significant way must be doubted. Regular churchgoing is said to be restricted to about 3 per cent. Anyway, in the words of the museum guide: 'The great difference between the interiors of our medieval and post-Reformation churches is the dominating place the pulpit takes in the latter, corresponding to the new importance of the sermon in liturgy. The importance of the three main elements of the service—the baptism, the sermon, and the officiating at the altar—is shown in the commanding position and the splendid decoration of the baptismal font, the pulpit and the altar piece.'

It is in the country churches, perhaps, that folk art and high art most nearly coalesce, for no doubt the best available craftsmen were used, some of whom would have travelled, and judged their own

Page 17 *Bergen: (above)* 1 *a view of the inner harbour and market place, the heart of the city, with Mount Fløyen behind. The Hanseatic Museum (page 12) is the third and lower of the three houses immediately behind the boats on the left edge of the photo; (below)* 2 *one of the many narrow streets of old wooden houses on the slopes of Mount Fløyen behind the Mariakirke (page 24)*

Page 18 (above) 3 *Hardangerfjord in spring. The combination of fruit blossom, fjord and snow mountain is 'one of the sights of Scandinavia' (page 26); (below) 4 the Stalheim Hotel, Jordalsnuten and the Naerøy valley. The road descends over 1,000ft from the hotel to the bottom of the valley in thirteen hairpins cut into the one steep slope (page 32)*

work by European standards. And Norway has a wealth of folk art, especially wood carving. We found that most of the churches contain delightful examples of this. So whatever your religious beliefs, do not ignore the churches. It may be difficult to catch one open, but if the attempt is made sufficiently often, you will gain an insight into one important way through which the creative spirit of a whole nation has expressed itself over several centuries, and still does.

In Bergen the oldest church is the Mariakirke, or St Mary's, up from the quayside at the top of Dreggen. A Catholic church of course until the Reformation, the architecture is massive Romanesque, for it was begun in the first half of the twelfth century. It is the only one to survive of the dozen or so churches of this period that the city once possessed. In it there is a fantastic pulpit of the seventeenth century, painted and most intricately carved. It is said to be the richest baroque pulpit in Norway. It was presented by the German Hansa, whose parish church this was. The altar tryptych is also German, and older. According to a guide who, during our visit, was perplexing a party of Americans with raw facts, it is painted with 22-carat gold.

Below the church there is a statue of Snorri Sturluson. When we passed he had a red pencil stuck in his belt, which seemed appropriate for the greatest of the Icelandic Saga writers. He is supposed to have attended mass at the Mariakirke before returning to Iceland and his murder in 1241.

Close by the Historical Museum are the Maritime Museum and the Museum of Natural History. We examined the former, because on being turfed out of the Historical Museum at 2 pm when it closed (as does the Natural History Museum) we found the Maritime Museum open for another hour. The Maritime Museum aims 'to provide a survey of the development of our shipping from ancient times right up to the present day'. It does this chiefly by means of models, and it will certainly be of interest to those who are fascinated by model ships. Like all Norwegian museums, it is beautifully laid out, uncluttered, clean, well lit.

B

Norway has for long been one of the world's great seafaring nations, out of all proportion to the size of its population. Possibly one need look no farther for an explanation than at a map of the country. The coastline, as measured round each inlet and fjord, is 17,000 miles, and this is shared by a population that in 1971 was still short of four million. There are 150,000 islands and innumerable lakes. Familiarity with water and boats is the birthright of almost every Norwegian child.

Norway has the world's fourth largest merchant fleet (2,847 ships of over 100 gross tons in July 1973), after Liberia, Japan and Great Britain. Most of this tonnage is employed on foreign trade, on charter, earning a very high proportion of the currency needed for the nation's imports. Tankers, passenger ships, bulk and ore carriers, and the fishing fleets form the greater part. None of this is government controlled or subsidised.

Bergen has always been a cosmopolitan port, linked to the world by the sea lanes of its merchant ships. The evidence for this is not to be found in Vågen, which is confined to passenger traffic and the local fish, vegetable and flower markets. But from Mount Fløyen can easily be seen where so much of the city's prosperity lies concentrated: in the docks and shipyards along Puddefjord and the inlets to the south. There are other industries: canning, a brewery, textiles and clothing, cod-liver oil, varnish and paint, margarine, chocolate, dairy produce, cattle foods, and so on. Bergen's commerical and tourist life are important, but ships and fish are the core of it, and the Maritime Museum its mirror.

We visited Rasmus Meyer's collection of paintings (mainly), furniture and interior decorations, housed in a building specially devised for them. It is described in the English catalogue as the most considerable collection of nineteenth-century Norwegian paintings and drawings outside Oslo's National Gallery. And it is an example of a phenomenon quite common in Norway, a collection built up privately by an individual and later presented to the public.

Rasmus Meyer, a businessman, lived from 1858 to 1916. He set out consciously to acquire a representative collection of the work of his countrymen. What is more unusual perhaps, he also bought pictures by contemporary artists, so that, for example, there is a whole room devoted to Edvard Munch, who was five years younger than Meyer. If you cannot get to Oslo, the thirty-two Munch paintings and the dozens of his prints and drawings will give you a good notion of his earlier work. I went to see Munch, but left impressed by other painters, especially by Harriet Backer, Nikolai Astrup, Gerhard Munthe, and by the prolific father of Norwegian painting, J. C. Dahl (1788–1857). Do not ignore Norwegian painting unless you ignore all painting.

In Bergen there is also the Municipal Art Museum, and a Fine Arts Society with exhibitions of contemporary art; a Museum of Arts and Crafts, a Fishery Museum, an Agricultural Museum, an aquarium, and a Leprosy Museum. It was a citizen of Bergen, Armauer Hansen, who in 1873 isolated the leprosy bacillus.

Beyond the aquarium (which is interesting, but scarcely merits the extreme praise of the guidebooks) is the Nordnesparken, a pretty headland not much visited by tourists. It has large trees, grassy banks, plenty of seats, and the sea glittering between the trees on two sides. It is a good spot from which to watch the ships in the fjord and to be at peace. Near the point there rises, improbably, a totem pole, genuinely carved from a tree trunk by a modern artist. If we puzzled out the tablet correctly, the pole was presented in 1970 by the city of Seattle, which has a considerable colony of Norwegian-Americans, to commemorate the 900th anniversary of the founding of Bergen.

Five miles out to the south of Bergen in the suburb of Hop is Troldhaugen, the home for the last twenty-two years of his life of one of Bergen's most famous citizens, the composer Edvard Grieg (1843–1907). The house has a charming Victorian air inside and out, which is not surprising, for Grieg had travelled extensively, and was at the peak of his fame during the high Victorian decades of the late nineteenth century.

The rooms of the house are as crammed with mementoes as a jackdaw's nest. It would take some time to study them adequately.

We had the misfortune to coincide with two coach-loads of visitors, mostly from America, who filled in turn each of the three rooms into which the guide crammed us. Only by staying behind when the crowd moved on was it possible to look around.

The grounds are beautiful, running steeply down to a lake. They are covered in a controlled wilderness of trees and shrubs, ferns, mosses, wild flowers and rock, and always the water glitters below. Several paths traverse through them: one leads down to Grieg's grave, and that of his wife, set in a perpendicular rock-face not far from the water; another leads to the hut on the hillside above a further stretch of water, where Grieg retreated to compose.

Despite an international training Grieg became a 'nationalist' composer. He derived much of his inspiration from the folksongs and dances of Norway which others had by then begun to collect and publish. This was a deliberate choice. National pride, the awakening of peoples all over Europe to a sense of self identity, is for good or ill at the heart of much recent European history and often proved a happy catalyst of the arts. Yet Grieg's music appealed everywhere and certainly helped to make Norway and the Norwegians known and appreciated beyond Scandinavia at a time when they were the junior and unwilling partner of a union with Sweden.

Incidentally, each year around late May and early June for two weeks an international festival of music, drama and folklore is held in Bergen.

There are many fjord excursions on offer. The nearer fjords are attractive but not spectacular; it seems scarcely worth visiting them unless you have no chance to sample fjords elsewhere. Longer trips take you farther afield in larger boats and into more spectacular parts. We had been tempted by a whole-day journey up the Sognefjord to Flåm, then up the famous branch railway-line to the junction at Myrdal, and so back to Bergen on the main Oslo-Bergen line. This should be a good excursion, though costly, and avoids the boredom of returning by the same route. If you take a boat trip, allow time to choose your seat, under cover or not, port side or starboard.

Our last Bergen visit was to a stave church, the *stavkirke* at
Fantoft. We had meant to inspect Old Bergen, and to poke around
inside the other city churches, and to motor out on the minor roads
to the west to get a feel of the guardian islands, where some of the
richest finds from Stone Age settlements have been found. But
there was no time. There is never enough time.

The Norwegian stave churches are unique, and I shall return to
them later (see especially pages 42–3). There really is nothing like
them elsewhere. None survive unaltered, yet most are worth
inspecting. *Stav* means a staff, stick, upright beam, pole or mast. A
stavkirke is a wooden church, built around a cubic framework of
vertical and horizontal beams, with walls of standing planks or logs
that bear no load.

This particular example at Fantoft, black from the layers of
preservative, was originally built in the twelfth century at Fortun in
the Sognefjord district, where it had been much altered in the seventeenth and eighteenth centuries. It was moved to Fantoft in 1884,
and very freely restored. It now has a stepped and steeply-pitched
roof of hand-carved shingles, great columns of whole tree-trunks,
carved dragons silhouetted high on the gable ends, and a peppering
of little shingled turrets. There are no windows. The general feel is
faintly reminiscent of a pagoda.

Bergen is a magic city. Many people have felt this. There are
some cities that immediately enchant the visitor. Bergen is one of
these. In recent years it has spread where it could along the edges
of the fjords and lakes and up the lower slopes of the surrounding
hills. But perhaps just because water and mountain have directed
this expansion in odd strips and patches away from the central core,
that core has retained its charm. From any street there is generally a
view of water or hillside, and twentieth-century concrete boxes
have not yet seriously impaired eighteenth-century grace and
nineteenth-century gravity.

One needs a week in Bergen. But whatever the time available, use some to walk in the back streets. Behind Bryggen, for example, is one of the older parts of the town, and the streets rise steeply, quiet and attractive, with painted wooden houses, unexpected alleys, flights of steps and sudden views down over the harbour (*plate 2*). Another area for exploration on foot is the ridge that stretches from the aquarium right through to and around the university. There are some charming quiet hotels up here.

Bergen is not typical of Norway, and it is perhaps sad that for so many visitors it is the only Norwegian city or town they see. But then no city is typical of Norway, for Norway is not a country of cities. It is significant that so many of its towns were deliberately founded by some king as an individual act of will. Until the industrialisation of the twentieth century, towns did not often evolve naturally. But if Bergen is not typical of Norway, it is none the less a good place to spend time in.

2 Bergen to Kaupanger

It was good to be on the move. Bergen had been rewarding to explore. Yet we had been chafing. The roads of Norway lay ahead and we were impatient to be on them. Now in the afternoon we were away, our motorcaravan fully loaded with food, water, petrol and a Welsh couple, newly married, who had landed at Bergen airport that morning. They had not been into the city. They were intent on reaching Oslo in the shortest space of time, and after Oslo, Greece—they had a hunger for perpetual motion. In the late afternoon we decanted them at Norheimsund, and ourselves turned off the E68 on to route 551.

From Bergen to Norheimsund had been 56 miles of tough driving, the road scarcely free of twists, with bouts of hairpins and tunnels, and mostly a rotten surface that shook us cruelly. Much of this stretch was being 'improved'. We were to learn later that roads being improved are most to be feared. For work proceeds cautiously. First the old surface is torn away and a winter or two is allowed for softening up the base. When this is full of potholes and rift valleys, work may begin; but only with caution, in short stretches and for limited periods. It is a triumph to be noted in diaries if one catches a road-making team on the job. Lack of money must be the reason, though I like to think that perhaps there are still people in the world who simply do not give a damn for the internal combustion engine.

If sections of those miles of E68 were rough, they were also

beautiful, revealing a splendid succession of fjords, lakes, waterfalls
and mountain passes. Every road in Norway is beautiful. And
perhaps now or next year that stretch will be transformed into
smooth tarmac.

Distinctly weary we searched for a side track up or down which
to halt. We wanted a night away from organised camp sites. A great
advantage of the motorcaravan, we had read, is that you can sleep
wherever you halt and can halt wherever you like. This is true. But
there are limitations: they are set by geography, the law, and
personal taste. Forty-five-degree slopes are uncomfortable. We
declined main-road lay-bys. The van must not block anybody's
right-of-way, or trespass too obviously on private property. We
looked for seclusion from people and seclusion from noise, together
with a view and running water. The water was not vital as we
carried a tank holding twelve gallons.

The 551 gave us a quite beautiful drive, a good dirt surface
winding beside the waters of the Hardangerfjord, with distant
snow-capped mountains beyond the green hills on the far shore. But
there was nowhere to park, no way off the narrow road except
down short tracks to houses. The banks of the fjord are closely
cultivated. Here in May and June the fruit blossom on the lower
slopes and the snow still thick above provides one of the sights of
Scandinavia (*plate 3*). In late July we saw plums and apples ripening,
raspberries under green nets, strawberries, and many sorts of vegetables. The area has a mild climate and good soil and no one wastes a
square foot of it.

In the end there has to be a compromise. The perfect camping
place is rare; or rather, can rarely be found in the time one is
prepared to spend looking for it after a day of driving and sightseeing. This, our first independent camp, seemed at the start not so
much a compromise as a defeat: 10 yards of flat grass and rock just in
from the road, hemmed by trees on three sides, without water, and
with houses 200 yards off. Yet it was good to be alone; city camp
sites are always crowded. Traffic on our road was thin, and ceased
altogether around 10 pm. No one came to stand and stare as

would inevitably happen anywhere in central and southern
Europe.

That evening there was some slight rain, our first. After the rain
and supper we walked, down the road and then steeply up a hill
track. Eventually this led on to grassland and magnificent views
over the Hardangerfjord to the mountains of the Hardangerjøkulen
and the Hardangervidda. It was about 9.30 pm yet still light, and
absolutely peaceful. Bergen had been absorbing but not peaceful.
Motoring is not peaceful. But the hillsides of Norway, and there are
thousands of square miles of them, are marvellously quiet and this
was our first taste of them.

After Bergen the next major objective was Trondheim, far to the
north. There are several routes that can be taken. We chose what
seemed to be the most direct. It follows the E68 to Voss and
Gudvangen, then by ferry to Kaupanger, by route 55 over the
Sognefjell to Lom and by route 15 to Otta, and then on the E6
north to Trondheim. This meant abandoning that enticing fjord
country to the west, the provinces of Sunnmøre and Nordmøre,
which from all accounts are superb. Florø, Ålesund Molde and
Kristiansund, Geiranger and the Trollstig Pass, these and so much
else must wait for another time. We should have riches enough, and
beyond Trondheim the Arctic Circle, Narvik and the Lofoten
Islands were on the menu.

The run next morning, 25 July, took us first along the north
shore of the Hardangerfjord. We had roused early and were rewarded by one of those still clear mornings that are like the birth
of the world. The waters of the fjord were motionless. At Norheimsund the white-painted houses along the shore, and the jetties
and small boats, were mirrored with extraordinary precision. Behind
them the green hillsides shone, and behind these the rolling mountains, grey and dark green, were fringed, where they met the sky,
with snow, white against blue. The road clings to the shore, though
often high above it, and the combination of mountain, fjord and

blue cloud-filled sky was irresistible. As always, the roadside was
alive with flowers, pouring from every patch of grass and every
crevice in the rock: willow herb, foxglove, scabious, blue harebell,
black bearberry, cinquefoil, vetch, clover and many others. There
were mosses on the rock, and ferns in profusion. The road surface
was good tarmac, though often narrow.

It was on this morning, when we stopped in solitude for breakfast
in a lay-by perched on a promontory about 100ft above the fjord,
that after a few minutes three beetle Volkswagens drew in with
military precision, and out of them emerged, like a conjuring trick,
twelve Swedes of all ages, a baby and a great complication of food
and drink. Within minutes the heavy wooden table on the site had
been wiped clear of moisture, there was a stove burning, twelve
plates had been laid, and then everyone was seated eating hot por-
ridge, surrounded by bread, jugs of milk, butter, jam, cheese and
drinks. We felt mildly ashamed of our bread and marmalade in the
hand and a mug of coffee balanced on the rear step.

Hardangerfjord is one of the great fjords. It runs north-east to
south-west, with its mouth towards the open Atlantic (or, as the
Norwegians sensibly call their share, the Norwegian Sea). At
latitude 60° it is well north of the northern tip of Scotland,
equivalent to the southern capes of Greenland, the centre of Hudson
Bay and south Alaska; but the Gulf Stream that keeps the polar
waters at bay, and the prevailing warm westerlies, have created a
climate that is mild by comparison. Also the rock that forms the
land edge of parts of the fjord is not the hard granite and gneiss that
make up much of western Norway; it is softer schist that has
weathered into more fruitful soil. Protected from strong winds and
from late frosts, the communities of the Hardanger, to an extent
rare elsewhere in the fjord country, can support themselves from
agriculture.

Nevertheless eastwards and inland Hardanger splits into half a
dozen subsidiary arms that are narrower and more typical of the
fjords. To the south, Sørfjord penetrates for 30 miles into the
mountain plateau; and at Kvanndal—where the ferry takes off for

Kinsarvik (one hour) and route 7's climb to the Hardangervidda and Oslo—we ourselves followed our E68 along the Granvinfjord and watched the mountains closing in, squeezing the water to a ribbon of blue.

From the head of the Granvinfjord over the pass to Voss is an easy and pleasant drive.* Voss is in a broad green basin at the head of a lake surrounded by hills. The centre of the town was bombed flat in 1940 and is therefore new. It is laid out on a grid pattern, pleasant but dull. Yet we liked Voss. It caught us in a good mood. Perhaps this was because the Information Centre had a nice washroom: lavatories loom large for campers and caravanners, who have no fixed base with conveniences to which they can retreat.

It was very hot. We inspected the church, which is thirteenth century onwards and escaped the bombs. The octagonal steeple of wooden timbers is original. The stone walls are $4\frac{1}{2}$ to 7ft thick. The interior is rich with colour and full of interest, well worth examining in detail with the aid of the English leaflet.

There is a cable-car and chair-lift up Mount Hangur, 2,780ft. By moving around over the rock, turf and bare peat at the top you can find a selection of views, and there is obviously good walking to the north and west. But there was a disappointing lack of flowers. The most obvious plant, common throughout mountain Scandinavia and much of Europe, was cotton grass. Cotton grass likes boggy places and sandy soils. There are several species. At this season, when in fruit, it is attractive and unmistakable, for the fruit are accompanied by dense tufts of pure-white bristles.

Voss is developing fast as a tourist centre for summer and winter. It has the advantage of being on the railway, accessible from Bergen or Oslo, and must be a convenient base for touring by foot, car, bus or rail. But Norway can offer more beautiful spots.

For our part the hot afternoon was passing and we had time for

* There is an alternative route from Bergen to Voss that we followed in 1973. This is route 13, which leaves the E68 at Trengereid, 25 miles out of Bergen, and arrives at Voss from the west. It is an equally beautiful road, but more rugged and mountainous, shorter but slower.

only one further item. It was sad to abandon a sight of Finneloftet, described so alluringly in one guidebook as 'Norway's oldest profane wooden building', and in another as 'a banquet hall for noblemen'. We chose the folklore museum at Mølster. This is a set of farm buildings, two farms in fact, as originally built and in use until 1926. The buildings date from various times, for the families grew in size and wealth. The oldest is c1500 and the youngest c1850. Inside they are furnished with local implements and handmade furniture of all periods. Living museums of this kind are to be found throughout Norway. Mølster is a typical example, and I will mention briefly a few items to be seen there, things that especially interested us among the 8,000 objects catalogued.

Until recent times everything for the home and farm was made on the spot or close by. Farmers and fishermen led isolated lives (many still do); they formed a thinly spread population scattered along the edges of the fjords and the narrow inland valleys, cut off from one another by difficult mountain country. Communities relied on themselves to a degree that it is no longer easy to appreciate. And they used the materials to hand, stone and wood, especially wood. An occasional travelling craftsman might introduce fresh ideas and perhaps set some new standard of skill. A change of resident official might bring to the area a chest-of-drawers from Copenhagen or a silver dish from Amsterdam, or copies of such pieces by craftsmen in Bergen or Oslo. But most things were made locally, by each family for itself. Distinctive shapes and patterns evolved from valley to valley: here in Voss a beer jug or a cart would not look quite the same as in Gudbrandsdalen or Setesdalen.

In the oldest room at Mølster the floor is of great slabs of slate as big as five or six London paving stones. There are enormous cauldrons hanging over the central hearth and a louvered hole in the roof for the smoke. There is a lantern made from a sheep's bladder, and a round stone, thin and some 4ft in diameter, for baking a kind of flat bread that could be stored for months. There are candlesticks (some of human height), each made from a branching fir. A bough is chosen that has divided into three smaller branches; these are cut off a few inches from the parent bough and form a tripod base. The main bough is hollowed out to receive the mutton-fat candles and slots are cut at intervals so that as the candles burn down they can be wedged higher. Simple and effective.

In this room there are platforms high at one end for sleeping. In other rooms there are the more sophisticated boxbeds, short, with straw mattresses and thick pillows; people slept half sitting. Skis and snow shoes are home made. In the girls' summer quarters above the byre there are painted chests for storing clothes, and several designs of wooden chair and stool. In a seventeenth-century room the vast table has whole tree-trunks for legs. The table is laid with wooden plates each with an individual mark and in a rack on the wall there is a row of wooden spoons. There are butter moulds and a cheese press, a wooden cradle that rocks, and a spinning wheel. Brightly coloured weaving—bed covers, wall hangings, clothes—is much in evidence, often with bold geometric designs.

Mølster lies high on the steep hillside behind Voss. Look along any of the great inland valleys of the southern half of Norway and notice how many of the older farms are similarly sited, half-way between the fertile river terraces and the huts of the high summer pastures, the *seter*. To these pastures, as soon as the snows had melted, the cattle were driven, just as they are in central France, in the Alps and in the Himalayas. But there is another reason for this hillside siting: by it the farms escape the severe spring frosts that can lie like a deadly gas in the valley bottoms. You may notice too how in east-west valleys the south-facing slopes may be intensely cultivated while those facing north may be left to forest.

The drive along the E68 from Voss to Gudvangen is very fine, past lakes, through wooded gorges and then, after 22 miles, reaching Stalheim. We had been looking for a campsite on the shore of Lake Oppheim, but missed it, and sooner than expected found ourselves at the Stalheim Hotel. We were hot, tired, thirsty and had eaten nothing but a slice of suicide cake on top of Mount Hangur since

that 8.30 breakfast.* We could not face the descent that lay ahead
without a break. So we went into the hotel, camouflaged by several
bus-loads of smart Americans.

The hotel is modern. But the attraction for us was the view from
the terrace at the back. The terrace is exactly on the edge of a drop of
over 1,000ft. From it you look down to and along the narrow,
winding gorge of the Naerøy valley; at the blue river, the road, a
few green fields, a couple of toylike farms, all sharing a ribbon of
flat strand between the towering rock walls of the mountains that
rise far higher than the hotel. Almost opposite is one very distinctive
mountain, the conical Jordalsnuten, bare rock from base to summit,
and for us a beautiful pink in the evening light (*plate 4*). No one
should drive past this view: it is of the top class and can only be
appreciated fully from the hotel terrace.

The road descent from hotel to valley is slightly alarming. One
book calls it the steepest in Norway. There are thirteen tight
hairpins one close after another, a rough gravel surface and a gradient of 1 in 5. First we were held up by a stalled French car on its way
up. A Volkswagen full of young Swedish men almost lifted it to the
top. Then we came face to face with an enormous bus on the second
hairpin. We had to back steeply up and on to the wrong side of the
road to give the bus space to sweep round. It was a relief to reach
the bottom and to drift slowly along the short and very spectacular
run to Gudvangen and the head of the Naerøyfjord. We had
covered only 100 miles, but it was nearly seven o'clock.

Although Gudvangen has been a staging post for hundreds of
years, it is still small: a handful of houses and shops and a hotel. It
exists for the ferry. This is one of the ferries that is bookable and it
does get booked up at the height of the season. We could have had a
9.20 sailing that evening. But the trip down the fjord was too good
to perform in poor light. The first space next day was not until 5.25

---

* Suicide cake—actually 'survival cake', from a recipe found in a cookbook
for campers. It is stuffed with spices, dried fruit, cherries, brown sugar, and
cider. We had two, baked on 16 July, and still tasting good on the Lofoten
Islands in the second week of August.

pm. We settled for that, content to rest for a time in this marvellous spot.

The Naerøy valley down which we had just motored winds beside and around buttress after buttress of 3,000ft mountain, very narrow, a deep cleft in the plateau above. Suddenly the river empties quietly into the fjord, which fills the cleft ahead from bank to bank, and continues out of sight as a twisting ribbon of water. From over the lip of the cliffs at intervals waterfalls plunge, fed by snow patches, some of whose crusted edges we could see. Wherever the rock is not smooth or sheer there are shrubs and small trees, so that the valley is green, not barren.

It was nine o'clock next morning before the sun rose high enough to reach down to us, and then it left us again for half an hour while a length of taller ridge took its time to spin out of the way. There were sheep on the scree slopes behind. By midday it was hot again, though there was a breeze which from time to time caught at the waterfalls and blew them into sheets of fine spray, iridescent in the sun.

At 12.45 we packed up and, leaving the van by the ferry, took a picnic along an easy and very pretty footpath that borders the west shore of the Naerøyfjord. The path leads to the village of Bakka. This walk is to be recommended for as far as time allows. While motoring one cannot take in the Naerøy gorge; even the ferry moves too quickly. On foot there is time to savour, to see and remember the detail. I swam in the fjord. It was warm enough in the shallows, but cooled off desperately in the deep water.

The ferry glides down the fjord smoothly, quietly, but fast. All the ferries we used were like that, coming and going with a minimum of fuss and no waste of time. Passengers walk aboard ahead of the cars. We found a couple of stools on the open top deck, with views ahead and astern. Next to us sat Minerva and Erma from Rhode Island, part of a bus-load of elderly and indomitable American ladies 'doing' Scandinavia.

For an hour and a half we sailed down the fjord, with the fantastic cliffs towering on both sides, in shadow to port, in sunlight to starboard. The fjord takes sharp turns between the spurs of the cliffs so that the view is always changing; wild romantic scenery not from the imagination of some nineteenth-century watercolour artist, but real. There are numerous waterfalls, and just occasionally a hamlet or an isolated farm with a strip of sloping field tucked in under the cliffs—communities whose only sure physical contact with the rest of the world has to be by boat (though all of them seem to have electricity). At certain times of day and year there are said to be seals in this fjord, but we saw none.

Eventually the Naerøyfjord merges into the Aurlandsfjord, which is a little wider and breezier; and an hour later this joins the Sognefjord, wider still. At the head of the Aurlandsfjord lies Flåm, with that railway up to Myrdal already mentioned (page 22). In 13 miles this line rises 2,900ft with a gradient of 1 in 18. Our ferry stopped first at Revsnes on the southern shore, where some cars drove on to the road for Oslo, the other and older route to the capital from Bergen.* The rest of us crossed to Kaupanger on the north shore, where we spent the night. The sinking sun touched the waters of Sognefjord to the west with a lovely soft light; and it silhouetted the gentler rounded mountains, turned them into a border of dark hump-backed whales.

Sognefjord is a phenomenon even in a country that is stuffed with natural wonders. Look at a map and see how it eats inland for well over a hundred miles, its many tentacles cutting into the mountains north, south and east in a bewildering complication of narrow channels. Kaupanger is far from the sea, but Sognefjord with its eastern arms continues for many miles yet, dividing the great

* Twenty-eight miles up the Laerdal valley from Revsnes there is the stave church of Borgund, the best preserved and least changed of the more developed type. Anyone with an interest in these buildings should try to see it (as we did in 1973).

Page 35 *Urnes:* (above) 5 *stave church from the south-west. It is constructed wholly of pine-wood; much of it is around 800 years old* (page 41); *(below)* 6 *the carved panels on the north wall* (page 41)

Page 36 (above) 7 *Nigard glacier, with a corner of the Jostedal ice-cap behind* (*page 45*); (*below*) 8 *Sognfjell: snow, blue lakes and mountains. Our motor-caravan is in the foreground. The ridge in the right background is at least a mile* *away* (*page 48*)

ible for over a quarter of the country's exports, are even more directly at the mercy of world conditions than are most.

It must be an odd and perhaps unsettling experience to work in one of these industrial complexes, company towns, isolated in some deep valley, perhaps without sun for much of the day in summer and for whole weeks in winter. At Rjukan in Telemark, which we visited later, it is said that the valley is sunless for four months. The workers are drawn from throughout Norway, forming colonies of skilled industrialised strangers in a scattered peasant community.

Modern industry excepted, each of the great fjords has always been to some extent an independent entity. The mountains that enclose them have been like the walls of a prison (and in winter must seem so quite literally), until recent days barring all but the most limited land contact between one and the next. The sea on the other hand has been a highway, carrying trade and ideas not merely between fjords, but between the fjord settlements and the rest of Europe. The Hansa merchants in Bergen were only the most obvious and intrusive of such contacts. It is no accident that it was among the fjords that the independent chiefs of the early Middle Ages withstood most stubbornly the attempts at unification with east and north.

3 Kaupanger to Trondheim

Kaupanger is minute, but has the Sogn Folk Museum and a much restored stave church. We were away too early to catch either. *Kaupang, kaupung, koping* or *kobing* means 'buying field'—ie a market place. Our English 'shop' derives from the same source. There are several kaupangs in Norway.

The tarmac road to Sogndal crosses an isthmus between Kaupanger and the Sogndalsfjord, winding high through the pine woods that clothe the sides of the valleys. Sogndal is a small fjord port and a considerable centre for these parts. Most of the people are employed in farming, trade, a meat-packing plant, and tourism. Along the Sognefjord and its branches, as along most fjords, farms are generally confined to the marine terraces that emerged with the rising of the land, and to the soil of the river deltas at the heads of the fjords. A few farms cling precariously to terraces high on the hillsides; you can sometimes see ropeways connecting them to fjord-side tracks. Fjord farms are often too small for mechanisation, or for the production of surplus crops for cash.

We stayed in Sogndal only to buy food, then left eastwards on route 55. Soon this climbs the Årøy river gorge. The lower part of the gorge contains the Hells Falls (Helvetesfossen), which we spotted debouching into the river. They looked dramatic. We had not yet 'done' a good waterfall, so stopped and with some difficulty scrambled down through steep woods to the edge. They *were* dramatic—a roaring rocketing force of white-green water between narrow rock walls, and the spray cooling us and encouraging the mosses and the ferns at our feet to phenomenal growth. This is a salmon river. We searched for the salmon reverentially, for had not the Maharajah of Indore fished the river, according to the guidebook, and George IV of Great Britain.

Above the gorge the land flattens and the road skirts the hillside round Lake Hafslo, which was an aquamarine blue of great intensity. At Solvornsgalden there is a road to the right down to Solvorn, a fjord village, with on the opposite bank of Lustrafjord, Urnes stave church, the oldest datable *stavkirke* in Norway (1140–50, with parts that may be eleventh century). For architectural and art historians it is an important building. There is no road to it.

From Solvorn a motorboat crosses about every half hour in summer (Kr7 return). Then there is a steep climb for fifteen minutes up to the church, which is almost the highest building in this small, scattered and isolated community (*plate 5*). The church is made of pine, as were all stave churches. The exterior is unassuming, slim, nicely proportioned. On the north wall are four carved panels, two of them round a doorway shaped like a keyhole (*plate 6*). The carving on these panels is very fine, almost three-dimensional: serpents and beasts intertwine with each other in a complex rhyth-mic pattern of curves that is certainly of pre-Christian inspiration, and has become the exemplar of a style, the Urnes style, much studied.

Indeed these panels and all the surviving portals of stave churches are a major achievement of the art of the Romanesque period in northern Europe. A visitor does well to view them whenever he finds them mentioned in his guidebooks. The University Historical Museum at Oslo (page 145) has a fine collection.

The interior of Urnes is splendid, rich with colour, wood and ornament. The shallow carvings on the capitals of the columns in the nave are especially noteworthy. So is the early Romanesque calvary group above the chancel arch, a rare survival. The Lutheran Reformation in the sixteenth century, though it produced its own riches, was very destructive of earlier work.

Urnes did not escape restoration. In the seventeenth century the

pews, pulpit and altarpiece were added. Restoration was undertaken
in 1902, for by then the whole church was in bad repair. The
windows are eighteenth century. The gallery that once surrounded
the church has been removed except for the west porch. But both
inside and out more remains from pre-Reformation times than in
almost any other stave church; there is a feeling of age, of tradition,
as you wander about. And the site is beautiful, well chosen, for on
this spur the church is visible for miles from that ancient highway,
the fjord.

I have said a little about *stavkirker* on page 23. The earliest stave
churches may derive from pagan shrines of the late viking age, for
Christianity when it came to Norway was imposed on a society
with long-developed traditions and art of its own. Not all experts
agree about this. Most *stavkirker* seem to have been built in the
twelfth century. In their simpler forms they were common through
much of Scandinavia. In Sweden and Denmark they have gone,
destroyed accidentally or soon replaced in stone or brick as popula-
tions and wealth grew.

In Norway, where these stave churches reached their most
advanced development, thirty or so have survived more or less
complete out of the 5–600 or even more there must once have
been. As late as 1800 there were still ninety-five. A handful retain
something like their original form; others, such as at Ringebu
(page 124) and Lom (page 49), have been restored or enlarged
or altered but keep enough of their early form to be called
stavkirker. Their survival is probably due to Norway's comparative
poverty and to their location away from the richer lowland areas.
It is in the latter that one finds the Romanesque stone churches.

In Norway through the Middle Ages almost all building was in
wood, even in towns. There are exceptions, such as the Cathedral
and Bishop's Palace at Trondheim, the Akershus Castle in Oslo,
Bergen's Mariakirke, and country churches of the richer districts.
These were 'official' buildings. Wood was the material for most

building (and to a great extent continues to be outside the centres of towns). Wood was plentiful and close by; it is an efficient insulator and does not crack in frosts. It has good strength and elasticity compared with its weight. It is easily carved.

Stavkirker display a skill and imagination in the use of timber, in the architecture of wood, that appears to be unique in Europe. The surviving buildings possess 'a highly refined structural system' (Anker, 380) whose origins are still the subject of expert argument. Where they have not been altered, the old brown roofs rise in diminishing tiers, leading the eye upwards to a belfry and perhaps a final thin pole. Roofs and often the walls are sheathed with hand-carved shingles, like chain-mail (*plate 29*). A rectangle of massive beams forms the vertical supports, and rests on other horizontal beams, or sills, which in turn rest on blocks of stone. Thus damp, the great enemy of wooden buildings, does not penetrate from the ground. These beams and the wall plates (horizontal upper beams) and braces that lock them together form a rigid cube that supports the roof. The walls are not self-supporting (as a brick wall is) and bear no load.

There are, or were, outside galleries or ambulatories at ground level in most churches, perhaps acting as a meeting place in bad weather. The porches usually had elaborately carved pillars and surrounds. A few of these have survived *in situ;* some are in museums. There may be dragons or other symbolic beasts jutting from the gable ends. The church is dark inside, unless later enlargement has introduced windows. And it seems lofty, for the width is less than the height. The ranks of upright pillars, the several layers of arches above them disappearing into the gloom, and the bracing St Andrew's cross-struts, all give a sense of great strength. Parts of this interior woodwork may be carved, especially the capitals of the columns: human and dragon faces, stylised animals, twisted interleaving patterns of branches and leaves (often vines) are favourites. It pays to take a powerful torch into a stave church to explore the roof area with light.

Early *stavkirker* are simple naves; later ones tend to a complication that is quite bewildering, most impressive, and unlike anything to be seen in Europe.

Down by Gaupnefjord we branched off route 55 on to the track (route 604) leading north up Jostedalen towards the Nigard glacier. This road was truly narrow and very dusty, but smooth. For the first half of the 21 miles it twists through a gorge. There is room to pass another car only where passing bays have been made. Each car met makes a small crisis, with one or other reversing. An odd product of this slow progress (15–20 mph) was that for much of the way our van was preceded by a single wagtail flitting along the road in front. When one bird stopped, another took over. Wagtails performed for us like this on a number of occasions later.

A large-scale map will show that Jostedalen penetrates between the Spørteggbreen to the east, a small ice-cap that rises to nearly 6,000ft, and the Jostedalsbreen, the largest stretch of unbroken ice and snow in continental Europe. The highest part of the Jostedals-breen, over 6,500ft, is at this northern end. According to my elderly Baedeker (1963), the thickness of the ice is estimated at 1,300–1,600ft; it covers 385 square miles and there are twenty-six large glaciers descending from it. The ice is receding, as almost everywhere in Europe. Indeed, relieved of the enormous weight of ice that covered it during the Quaternary Ice Age, the whole Scandinavian peninsula is rising from 0·8in to 4in per decade.

Writing with hindsight, I should have arranged a time and a place for climbing the eastern wall of Jostedalen in order to achieve a panoramic view of the ice-cap. A half day might be enough. But throughout this first part of our journey we could never allow too many diversions, for I was determined to reach the Lofoten Islands with time to explore. So except for the Nigard glacier, we saw only edgings of ice, the lips and tips of the descending arms.

Jostedalen began to remind me more and more of certain valleys in the foothills of the Himalayas: great grey walls of rock, a rushing glacial river, patches of low scrub-like trees, and wherever the valley widened, lines and irregular heaps of round, grey-white stones, carried by past floods and worn smooth by friction. Occasionally an alluvial terrace supports a few fields of grass or crops, with a house or two and barns.

Eventually, beyond Gjerde, we arrived at an isolated, tall, square red house, a café, with a pleasant garden. Here tickets are sold for the toll road to the Nigard glacier. The glacier and part of the ice-cap behind it are in view (*plate 7*). The ice winds steeply down between rock. The valley leading to it is desolate: low scrub and acres of round stones, with occasional islands of short turf, and the creamy green river. In less than 2 miles there is a car park above a lake. From here you may boat or walk. The walk took us fifty minutes of slowish scrambling over rock and loose gravel, and across a number of small streams. The young and agile might save ten minutes. There is a trail marked by daubs of red paint. You need stout shoes (or at any rate not high heels, which were crippling one woman). It was hot. Yet immediately beneath the glacier there was a cold wind that demanded jerseys.

It is possible to join a guided party for a climb up the icefall of the glacier. This could perhaps be fixed on the spot (there was a group setting off as we arrived) and can certainly be arranged at Sogndal. Crampons are provided.

While clambering slowly towards the glacier a large ice cave becomes increasingly prominent. I ought not to have been surprised, but was, to find that from it there came roaring forth a really violent flood of water, the melt-water of the glacier. The cave was perhaps 50ft across and 30ft high. Its roof was blue. The water was greeny-white and every few minutes brought with it lumps of ice.

Glacial melt-water is interesting stuff, supporting a high density of finely-grated rock debris. It is this which gives to glacial streams their milky appearance. When the water loses momentum—in a lake for example—the debris sinks to form 'varved clays'. These are clays that alternate thick summer layers of this 'rock flour' from the glacier with thin winter layers, when the glacier is not melting, of darker organic material. The patterns vary from year to year, and com-

parisons of clays in various lakes have been used to date and map the
retreat of the last ice-sheet across northern Europe.

Glaciers acquire and transport huge quantities of rock debris:
debris that falls on to them from the frost-shattered ridges and
peaks above, and debris which the moving ice scrapes and gouges,
like a file, from the floors and sides of its valleys.* The piles of such
debris along the edges and at the snouts of glaciers are moraines.
The lake below the Nigard glacier occupies what no doubt is an
ice-gouged hollow. Many of Norway's lakes were formed by
moraine dams. In time the lakes will be refilled by the debris-
deposits of their feeder rivers.

Looking back down the valley from the snout of the Nigard,
which is 100ft or more above the lake, you see a very typical glacial
valley, shaped like a U, with a flattish bottom, steep sides that have
been scraped fairly clean of projecting spurs, and a mass of waterfalls
tumbling from the hanging valleys along the rims. Where debris
does not hide it, the bed-rock is smooth and rounded by ice action,
another typical sign of glaciation. This smooth rock makes good
walking. But near the Nigard glacier it is covered by a thin layer of
grit that is very treacherous.

It was 5 pm when we regained the car-park and time to look for a
camp. The few cleared spaces in the boulder wilderness beside the
track were already occupied, minute tents emphasising the desola-
tion instead of humanising it. We drifted down to Gjerde and
settled for an empty camp site beside the river. This turned out to
be a new site, uncompleted. The lavatories worked, but there was
no hot water. The washrooms smelt of freshly-sawn wood.

The owners of the site were stacking hay on to lines of wire in
the next field, and stayed at work until nearly 10 pm. A girl in a
two-piece bathing costume came over to warn us of the lack of hot
water. She spoke a little English and told us that the man employed
to build the huts had gone on 'walkabout'; otherwise the site would
by now have been ready. We had already learned that in summer

* A striking example of transportation of rock by ice is the presence in East
Anglia of rocks from Scandinavia, carried and deposited during the first ice age.

this can be a hazard for forward-planning. The winters are so gloomy, so restrictive, that when the short summers are in full spate some men have to break away, get out of the valleys, walk the mountains, fish the rivers.

The next day's drive was among the most beautiful of our journey. After rejoining route 55 we moved on good tarmac along the shores of Gaupnefjord and Lustrafjord, both arms of the great Sognefjord complex. Gaupnefjord was a deep green, Lustrafjord an intense blue. At Skjolden we left these western fjords for the last time. It was a sad moment. Now we were to strike inland for Trondheim. At Fortun (where there is a power station, and where Bergen's Fantoft stave church was originally built) begins the ascent to the Sognefjell over a mountain pass of great antiquity between the eastern valleys and the fjords. Across this pass, along what used to be a pack-horse track, corn grown in the dry eastern valleys was humped to the fjord settlements in exchange for salt that was produced by boiling sea-water. The modern route climbs from 985ft to 4,690ft up a narrow, zigzag dirt road. It is easier not to meet buses or tankers.

At Turtagrø (3,250ft) there is a mountain hotel, a famous centre for climbers and walkers. It is above the tree line, surrounded by moorland. From here you can reach a glacier in one and a half hours of walking, and from here a toll-road leads south over wild mountain country for 20 miles down to Øvre Årdal and its aluminium, another tempting diversion. We stopped some way above the hotel to look back down the gorge, and to savour the views of the Hurrungane mountains. There are two fine peaks about the 7,000ft mark, and others close to it.

The Hurrungane, and the Jotunheim mountains in general, are different from the mountains we had so far seen. Here for the first time were jagged peaks, sharp *arêtes*, the ridges, corries and precipices of a young mountain range unsubdued by ice, in contrast to the gentler rolling plateau on which we now rested and out of which the

peaks rise as from a sea. Indeed this is what they once did, only the
sea was ice, and the crumbling and cracking and splitting by frost
and by sun through those final ice-age summers are what made the
peaks jagged and the ridges sharp.

Walking through the low, wiry bushes on the hillside above
Turtagrø we came upon our first cloudberry (molte), a plant that
seems to hold a mystical fascination for Norwegians. It only grows
on the plateaux, and likes moisture. When the berries are ripe they
are hunted and harvested with almost religious determination.
Food stores always stock cloudberry jam. It is expensive and,
shamefully, we never bought it. Indeed we never came upon the
berries properly ripe (yellow), so could not taste the fruit. Less
than ripe, it is tasteless.

Turtagrø is a curtain-raiser, an hors d'oeuvre. The road goes on
climbing. After another 1,000ft or so it enters the Sognfjell, a
fantastic landscape, a vast plateau, not flat, with peaks, snowfields
and glaciers lining every horizon, and a multitude of lakes, small
and large, each a deep blue in contrast to the bordering patches of ice
and snow (plate 8). The rock outcrops when observed closely are
often mottled with lichens, brown, green and yellow. The moss
and turf between the rock carry flowers but are mostly clothed
with dwarf shrubs. I have not seen anything like this landscape.
There cannot be many parts of the world where scenery of such
grandeur is available to anybody of almost any age and state of
health for the price of a bus ticket.

We were lucky in the weather. We stopped somewhere in the
middle, put on boots and walked south into a burning sun. Beside
the road there were a lot of people taking picnics; few walked
away from the road. Yet it is easy walking, and exhilarating, with
these magnificent views in all directions. The snow was firm.
Sometimes there were extensive patches of dried moss which
crunched beneath boots like brittle ash. There was a cool wind,
but sheltered from this it was hot enough to sunbathe.

Near the Sognefjell Tourist Hut, close to the road's highest
point (4,690ft), we stopped again. There were three sheep lying

in the shade of a parked car, though there was ice floating on water close by. A man with a rucksack passed, driving a pack-horse. That is the way to travel this land.

The northern peaks of the Jotunheimen are the highest in Scandinavia: they are Galdhøpiggen and Glittertind, both just over 8,000ft. These are not great heights by world standards, but their northern latitude makes them formidable. Route 55, as it descends the Leirdal valley, passes close under Galdhøpiggen.

There is no space to linger on the rest of this drive. There are several more tourist stations near the road, and mountain huts among the peaks, and hotels lower down. It would be easy to spend days in the area. We ourselves descended almost to Lom, completing 81 miles, and stopped in an unstarred camp site, 'Sulheim Camping'. It was almost empty, a little primitive, but pretty, with silver birch round a green field, and a fine group of old farm buildings up the hillside behind (*plates 9 & 10*). In other fields nearby a tractor was turning the hay and a powerful jet spray was watering potato plants.

The weather changed next morning. We left in a drizzle and it was still drizzling at Lom, where route 55 joins route 15. Westward up the Ottadalen route 15 makes for the Nordfjord and the northern flank of the Jostedalsbreen. We turned eastward.

Lom is credited with the driest climate in Norway, so naturally we were not surprised to pass through in rain. It used to be a remote area little known or visited. Here there is a fine *stavkirke*, probably thirteenth century, a pillared basilica enlarged in the seventeenth century to a cruciform plan. The original roof-crest has been removed and is now in the Lillehammer museum. It has been replaced with a copy. There is an interesting door with carved flanking columns and arch in the north transept. But it is the interior that is impressive (open daily from 9 am to 9 pm). The columns rise through three levels of arcades and braces. The nave is broader than at Urnes. And the rich seventeenth-century additions and furniture make a fine whole. When we passed through Lom again in 1973, the nave floor was being excavated, so there may now be fresh evidence of the church's early history and on the origin of *stavkirker*.

We pushed on for Vågåmo, 20 miles away. By fjord standards the valley is wide, with wooded flanks and little visible rock. There is pasture and an abundance of cows, and farms with large barns, all revealing a prosperity which the west coast, generally, cannot match. These were the first cows we had seen.

At Vågåmo the rain stopped. We parked by another stave church. This was rebuilt as a cruciform in 1630, when a wooden tower and spire were added, but the interior has lost almost all its original character, and is now pleasant seventeenth-century work. Outside there is a separate bell tower, square, solid and tall—a log cabin with ambitions. It is about forty logs high. The door in the south transept is from the original church, as is the attractive blind arcading on the west front. The churchyard, like almost all Norwegian churchyards, is beautifully kept. None of the graves is neglected; each has its shrubs and flowers. As a consequence church-yards are gay. They are also good for picnics, for they have seats and usually a water tap somewhere.

We decided to look at the Håkenstad farm museum about $1\frac{1}{2}$ miles up the mountainside to the north-west on another lovely site. It proved to be an interesting contrast to the Mølster farms at Voss, richer, with elegant sixteenth- and seventeenth-century interiors holding many imported luxuries. The exteriors are carved and painted, with covered galleries. I was fascinated as always by the texture of the wood and the way it is joined together, and the smell and feel of it. Wooden buildings are nearly all beautiful, however rough.

At Håkenstad four rooms only are on show. Three of them are in the same building, which has a small bell-tower above the main door, a feature of the farms in this region. The fourth room is the still-used living-room of the main house. Håkenstad is occupied. Everything on display belongs to the farm and was once in use.

The road from Vågåmo to Otta descends gently for 270ft and 24 miles through pinewoods and beside the rapids of the Ottaelv. Otta itself was a maelstrom of people and cars. It is, of course, an important road junction, twice the size of Lom and Vågåmo. It is an indication of how the emptiness of Norway had already changed our attitudes that Otta, with its population of 2,000, seemed like a metropolis. We took petrol aboard and moved out, north along the E6, the Arctic Highway.

We were now in the upper part of the great Gudbrandsdal valley, over 100 miles long, which in the opposite direction leads straight to Lake Mjøsa and Oslo. It was down Gudbrandsdalen that the two ill-equipped, ill-supplied and unacclimatised Territorial battalions of Britain's 148th Brigade were hurried in April 1940; and it was back up the valley that they were forced to retreat in less than one crucifying week. At Otta was fought one of the very few successful battles of that bungled campaign, by the troops of the 15th Brigade, recently landed at Åndalsnes. But they fought without artillery support and virtually no air cover. These small-scale battles in a remote theatre of World War II were of no importance, yet to the author, an ex-infantryman of that war, though on another continent, they have a gloomy fascination. And to the men involved they were as critical as any battle anywhere.

The main railway from Oslo to Trondheim follows Gudbrandsdalen, and not far to the north of Otta both road and rail must cross the barrier of the Dovre mountains, the range that divides the northern half of Norway from the southern half. But before crossing these we meant to spend a night in the Rondane mountains to the east.

An English writer has called the Rondane 'one of the most hauntingly beautiful parts of the entire country' (Hay, 91). North of Otta there are several roads leading to it. From the description each sounds entrancing. We chose the most northern since it is a through road.

The E6 was unpleasantly full of traffic. Our road, a toll road, took off from it at Dovre, and was empty. It twisted very steeply

and excitingly up the eastern flank of Gudbrandsdalen, first through
cultivated fields, then through rough pasture, and finally on to open
moorland. We had come to appreciate these quick ascents into the
hills, and to search them out deliberately. Dovre is at 1,590ft;
the toll gate is about 7 miles on at around 3,750ft, but most of the
climbing is done in the first 2 miles. Nearing the top, in patches of
open grass among low birch forest, there were sheep. Up on the
moorland there was not much grass; the ground tends to be
covered with a layer of wiry shrubs, varying in height from a few
inches to a couple of feet, not always easy to move through and
presumably useless to domestic animals.

Beyond the toll gate the road deteriorated. It was badly rutted
and with holes. But it was navigable in low gear, and the scenery
becomes increasingly interesting. There is a point not far on where
the road drops sharply to a section of the Grimsdal, deep and
totally enclosed. It was like discovering some lost world. The sense
of isolation was intense, perhaps increased by the cloud that was
settling lower. The valley floor was green and flat and along it the
Grimsa river meandered crazily, an immense agitated snake. A high
cross-ridge blocked the far end.

The river drops from terrace to terrace in giant steps. We passed
several *seter*, apparently empty, and then the Grimsdalshytta, a
collection of buildings high on a hillside to the north, a walking
centre. About 5 pm we followed a short track off the road that led
through some old gravel workings to a spot close to the river and
partly sheltered by a grassy bank. Here was home for the night.

We were at the centre of a wide circle of hills, a scene of lonely
grandeur in the stormy weather that was upon us. There were a
few uninhabited huts three-quarters of a mile off. At long intervals
a car passed slowly down the road, each one raising the fear that it
might stop and disturb our solitude. Otherwise no sight or sound of
humans.

Later the rain gave up and we strolled down the valley. The
variety of lichens and mosses was striking. In one place, on a low
hill, we walked only on lichens, pale primrose yellow, light green

Page 53 (above) 9 *a group of old farm buildings at Sulheim, Bøverdalen, near Lom (page 49). Note the bell tower and the slate roofs. In some valleys turf roofs predominate; in others, slate. The shape of the slates varies from valley to valley; (below) 10 an old house at Sulheim, with reindeer antlers above the door*

Page 54 (above) 11 *hay draped over lines of wire to dry, Sognefjord area. A very typical summer sight. Generally the ground is too damp and the showers too frequent for stooking; (below) 12 a forage harvester (page 115) on the rich farm lands between Kongsberg and Drammen. Most farms of any size now have one of these*

and dark green, all with the most delicate and intricate formation of miniature branches. There was a long hillside across the river that was ablaze with the yellow sort even in this dull evening light.

By 10 pm the angry clouds had come lower. We left the front curtains off and lay in bed gazing at the view—river and gravel and shrubby plain in the foreground, hills appearing and disappearing in the distance. This was motorcaravanning at its most satisfactory.

If the weather in Grimsdalen had been kinder we might have stayed. But next morning the clouds were still low, so we set off as planned for Trondheim. We did 150 miles that day (Sunday, 30 July), the longest distance so far.

Our route rejoined the E6 at Hjerkinn, already at over 3,000ft. At the junction, on a bluff to the right, is Eystein church. It is a modern building, beautiful inside and out, and on a fine site. The Norwegians have been imaginative with their modern church building.

Just beyond the church and over a rise that is the highest point of the crossing (3,370ft) of the Dovre mountains, there is a distant view to the north-west of three snow summits, including Snøhetta (7,497ft), and of the wide expanse of the moorlands, of wilderness, leading to them that in winter must be desolate indeed. The absence of trees at this height is attested by the picnic tables and seats in the lay-bys—they are no longer made of great logs.

The Dovrefjell carries no glacier ice now, despite its height. This may be because of the low precipitation in this part of Norway. Glaciers need a great deal of snow with which to renew the summer melt.

From the pass the E6 starts a long descent, gentle and continuous for mile after mile. At Kongsvoll there is a botanical garden just north of the railway station, beside the track. It is small, about 40 yards by 15, enclosed by an open fence, and not locked. We found it useful for identifying at least some of the mountain flowers we had seen. The names are given in Norwegian and Latin and the latter provides the common ground with any English flora.

After Kongsvoll the road descends through a prolonged gorge.

D

Here, and for days afterwards as we drove north, the rosebay willow herb was a joy, often lining the road on both sides like a processional way, or stretching back in fields, or terraced up a hillside. Meadow sweet, white campion, and harebells also grew in profusion, and many other flowers.

The turf roofs of older Norwegian houses are well known. The turf acts as insulation, and it keeps in place the layer of water-proofing birchbark that covers the planks beneath. Usually such roofs are seen on single or two-storey buildings. It was somewhere along this stretch of the E6 that we passed a very tall isolated station building, wearing a turf roof like a frayed top hat. A few miles on we saw for the first time (though often later) small birch trees growing from turf on a roof. It is noticeable that the pitch of these turf-roofed houses is never steep. One reason for this is to keep the winter snow lying on the roof, for snow is also an insulator.

Nearing Oppdal the gorge opens out, and Oppdal itself is at the centre of a wide and oppulent basin, with more fields and more farms than we had so far seen. The leaflet from the information centre (which is open on Sundays) advertised the town as a great winter-sports centre. This was hard to believe on a really hot, even oppressive midday in late July. The centre seemed like a frontier town, all new, with wide spaces of dusty earth and an unfinished look to everything. It was crowded with tourists.

From Oppdal to Trondheim the surface and the grading of the E6 is extremely good, with the top limit of 50 mph possible most of the way. After Sokna the valley broadens and the road runs between and over broken hills, well cultivated, richer even than Oppdal. The land has become civilised. The traffic is heavy. It was good to drive down into the centre of Trondheim (at 3.25 pm) and to find the tourist office open.

4 Trondheim

Trondheim is a nice city, though it has not Bergen's beautiful setting nor Bergen's bustle. It appears placid. This latter verdict is probably a reflection of my own physical condition, for the weather was sultry, too hot for the effort of sustained sightseeing. One aspect of Norwegian life it is difficult for the summer visitor to grasp is that what he sees as green and blue, and feels, if he is fortunate, as hot, for much of the year is white, cold and hidden by the long nights. Conditions vary from south to north, but many people not only live in valleys from which the sun is cut off by mountain ridges and in a land blanketed by snow from perhaps November to May (*plate 20*); some live where there is no sun at all for a time and little for several months. The Norway of the smiling summer is very different from that of the midday night.

Trøndelag, the province of which Trondheim is the capital, is on the threshold of the Arctic. It is the link province between south and north Norway. This is perhaps the place to stress the obvious physical fact of Norway's length. A persistent crow flying from the North Cape down to Oslo, pausing there for an *aquavit*, and then flying south for a similar distance, would land up sipping *chianti* on the far side of Milan. Trondheim may seem a long way north to the southerner, but there are another 1,220 miles of road from Trondheim to Kirkenes. Trondheim is not in the Arctic, but it is a fair distance farther north than, say, Anchorage in Alaska.

Our first move after leaving the tourist office was to visit the cathedral. Trondheim as a town is considered to have been founded in 997 by Olav Tryggvason. In those days and for hundreds of years everybody in Norway was called either Olav or Harald. The confusion which this brings to the earnest foreigner is nicely illustrated here. The first cathedral was begun by King Olav Kyrre (the Peaceful, died 1093) as a shrine to St Olav (Olav Haraldsson 995–1030), who was killed a few miles north of the town at the Battle of Stiklestad on 29 July 1030.

Olav Tryggvason was a great-grandson of Harald Fairhair, who attempted to master the whole of Norway and harried his rivals of the western fjords into emigration and settlement in Iceland. This is the Olav who, with the Dane Svein Forkbeard, besieged London and ruined the English King Ethelred. Somewhat later he seems to have adopted Christianity with that whole-hearted, rough and uncombed enthusiasm that characterises so much of viking achievement, though doubtless he did so from political as well as spiritual motives. He returned to Norway accompanied by English or English-trained priests and encouraged conversion from the old pagan rites with a liberal use of the sword and of torture. In Trøndelag he built a royal manor, a church and a market place in the loop of the river Nid where Trondheim now sprawls, and made them his base. But he had accumulated too many ambitions and too many enemies, both at home and abroad, and three years later died in a sea battle off Denmark.

Olav Haraldsson, the future saint, was another convert champion of the Christian faith. During his 'reign' (1015–28), a Church of Norway was organised on a lasting basis. He too had small patience with charity and tolerance as methods of conversion, and he too antagonised people at home and abroad.

But his death at the Battle of Stiklestad, at the hands of an army composed chiefly of local men, was followed by an extraordinary reversal of feeling. He had been heartily hated by most of his countrymen, many of them Christian. A year later he was being acknowledged a saint, his body incorruptible. It was still visible and well preserved in the seventeenth century. St Olav became Norway's patron saint, a symbol of national independence. His influence spread: London has had at least six churches of St Olave (one remains—St Olave, Hart Street, in the City), and there is still a St

Olave's Hospital, a St Olave's Grammar School, and roads named St Olaf and St Olave.

The founding of Trondheim Cathedral as a reliquary for the bones of St Olav drew pilgrims from all Europe. Trondheim expanded until it supported nine other churches and five monasteries, controlled the trade of the north, and for over two centuries was the spiritul and cultural centre of Norway, the chief residence of its kings and of a powerful archbishopric.

The city declined—commercially, because Bergen's Hanseatic merchants came to monopolise the northern fish trade (page 13), and politically and culturally, because after 1380 the Norweigan monarchy passed to Denmark, whose chief interests lay in the Baltic and in central Europe. Trondheim became a distant and unimportant outpost on the fringe of the world, decimated by the Black Death and abandoned by men of ambition. Present prosperity is comparatively recent, its slow beginnings dating from the middle of the eighteenth century. In 1800 the town had fewer than 9,000 inhabitants (Bergen 18,000; Oslo, 12,000). Yet it had always kept a remnant of its former splendour, perhaps in the minds of people rather than in any tangible form; and since Norway's independence, it is in Trondheim Cathedral—the Cathedral of Nidaros—and not in Oslo, that the kings have been crowned.

Nothing remains of the first cathedral. Its successor is a mixture of twelfth-century Romanesque and thirteenth-century Gothic in the Anglo-Norman tradition (there were close cultural relations between England and Norway at the time). I could admire without liking it. The general effect inside and out seemed to me heavy, short on inspiration, as though the techniques for erecting such a building were understood, but the spirit which should inform the techniques was missing or diluted. Perhaps the subsequent history of the building is partly the cause. After successive fires, and looting by the Lutherans at the Reformation (the saint's shrine and most of the cathedral's treasures were removed and lost), the cathedral was in ruins by the early eighteenth century. There was talk of pulling it down. Much of what is seen today is nineteenth- and twentieth-

century restoration, especially the nave and west front. Although
the work of restoration 'has attracted to its service some of the
country's best architectural and artistic talents' (Popperwell, 29),
possibly they too have not been happy working in the Gothic mode.

On behalf of the cathedral and those who have laboured to
restore it to something like its medieval glory, I have to confess
that we saw it under less than ideal conditions. The precinct was
seething with fellow tourists. We were tired after a long day of
driving. And we arrived at 4 pm to find that on Sundays the place
closed at 4 pm. Actually the barbarian hordes were still pouring
through the west door. We poured with them to an interior so
dimly lit that it was quite impossible to make out detail or even,
in places, where to put one's feet. Our hurried and stumbling canter
through the gloom was not fair to the place, which looks impressive
in photographs. I meant to go back, but never did.

South of the cathedral lies the fortress-mass of the Archbishop's
Palace, a medieval building of about 1200, whose exterior walls are
like enormous jig-saw puzzles, beautifully put together with stones
of all shapes, sizes and colours, pierced at infrequent intervals by
minute round-headed windows. Whoever ordered this building
did not feel at ease in his world. Whoever built it had an eye for
pattern and colour that would delight contemporary abstract
artists.

Beyond the palace (there are conducted tours of the interior
during the summer) beside the Elgeseter bridge, you can descend
to a riverside park that curves with the bend of the river northwards
until the next bridge, Bybrua (bru = bridge), is reached. In this park
was a nice example of the fact that an English-speaking visitor can
understand many of the public notices. A large board beside the
grass proclaimed FOTBALLSPARKING FORBUDT. Other examples from
Trondheim: HARDKOKT EGG (on a menu); INNGANG NESTE DØR (in a
shop window); PARKERING FORBUDT (almost everywhere).

From Bybrua there is a good view of the river fronts of the old
warehouses (from 1708) lining the Nid northwards to the next
bridge. They are partly built out over the water on piles. The

painted vertical planking makes solid blocks of patterned colour—
pale yellow, ochre, rust red, light and dark browns, blue, grey—
that are reflected faithfully in the water. Walking along Kjøpmanns-
gata behind the west-bank warehouses you can see what a massive
affair each is, stretching back a great many yards, often broad and
five or six storeys high. Like the Hansa houses in Bergen, these
Trondheim warehouses illustrate the Norwegian builder's un-
obtrusive mastery of the architecture of wood.

It was late. We left the city on the road to the north to prospect for
a camp site, and found Storsand Gard at Malvik, 12 miles out. The
site was crowded, with a railway track in a cutting along one edge
and a whistle point opposite our patch. On the other hand Strind-
fjord was a hundred yards away, with a rocky beach and oyster-
catchers feeding and calling in the evening light.

We both achieved much-needed showers. The water in mine
had gone cold, a little too bracing at the time, but wonderful
afterwards. The bashful should be warned: campsite showers for
men seldom allow individual privacy. The women, I am told, are
presumed to be more modest.

It was a morning of 'make and mend' next day. I had a sea bathe.
The water was cool, but no cooler than the English Channel most
summers, and the sun was hot.

At this kind of camp site many of the residents are here for long
periods, with TV sets, flower baskets, canvas fences around their
territory, and a mass of ancillary equipment. The tents and caravans
are packed close together. The best sites overlooking the beach are
more or less permanently taken. One-night standers such as ourselves have to fit where they can in the distant suburbs. We never
saw a GB car here, or heard English spoken, which was satisfactory.

We spent part of the afternoon in the Royal Norwegian Scientific

Society's Museum on Erling Skakkes gate in Trondheim. The society was founded in 1767 and has been an important influence on the intellectual development of Norway. For fifty years, for example, it was the only centre of learning in the country above the level of the four ancient cathedral schools. The museum, like Bergen's Historical Museum, is not too large and is well displayed. In addition to the prehistoric and historical sections (with another fine collection of medieval and Renaissance altars and pulpits), there is one on natural history that includes a bird diorama. To enliven this there is a recorded commentary and a sample of each bird's song. While the song lasts a spotlight catches a stuffed singer of the species crouching in the grass or on a branch.

The centre of Trondheim is undistinguished but pleasant. The streets are broad, laid out in 1681 after one of the more disastrous of the early fires. They are lined now with a mixture of late nineteenth-century and early twentieth-century stone commercial buildings, a few traditional houses of wood, and some twentieth-century international matchbox jobs. At the intersection of the two principal streets, the Munkegata and the Kongensgate, there is a large square, Torget, where Olav Tryggvason's statue caps a tall column which forms the pointer of a huge sundial, with a compass in the roadway below.

Part of Torget is a market place. In summer the vegetables, fruit and flowers are balm to the eye. Probably most of the fruit is grown locally. At any rate on our return from the north, we reached Trondheim by an early ferry across the fjord from Vanvikan, and on the ferry were a smartly dressed woman and small boy with sixteen large flat boxes of blackcurrants. Later we saw them on the fringe of the Torget market, their boxes piled on the pavement.

Munkegata runs from the cathedral through Torget down to the inner harbour, Kanalhavn, where there is a fish market, Ravnkloa (the fish is not cheap), and a small quay from which the sightseeing cruises in motorboats seem to take off. It is an attractive street, lined with trees and wide pavements. It is in Munkegata, not far from Torget, that you can see Stiftsgården, perhaps the largest wooden building left in Europe, dating from 1774–8, 'a fine example of provincial Palladian as it was interpreted in Norway' (Paulsson, 152), and the residence of the king when he is in Trondheim. There are conducted tours round it.

Even central Trondheim is not all wide streets. There remain some narrow passages. And beyond the centre there are many streets of modest wooden houses, two and three storeys, mostly painted ochre, pale yellow or white. The predominating ochre and pale yellow give such streets a pleasantly dusty, lazy, rather down-at-the-heel atmosphere in sunlight, and a faint melancholy in rain. They are an unexpected contrast to the strong colours of the old warehouses by the river and of the farmhouses in the surrounding countryside. I found them attractive. Moreover parking there is easier and cheaper (in the centre, one hour for one krone; a little farther out, two hours for one krone).

The central waterfront at Trondheim is a disappointment, in contrast to Bergen. Most of it is inaccessible, taken up with ware-houses and other buildings of commerce. The city ends along Kanalhavn. Between this and Trondheimsfjorden are two islands entirely devoted to railways and docks.

There is a good deal to see in and around Trondheim. We chose the Ringve Museum of Musical History, laid out in one wing of a seventeenth-century hill-top manor house in the eastern suburbs. The former owner of the house and his wife conceived the idea and carried it through. Another wing was being converted to a concert hall. About twenty of us were taken round by an enthusiastic bilingual student (male) who was himself able to play many of the instruments, and did so, and could joke in two languages. Most of the rooms are decorated and furnished in the period of a particular composer, and abound with paintings, photo-graphs and other mementoes; it is another example of the Nor-wegian talent for giving life to the past.

But it is the musical instruments that must be the chief attraction. They are not confined to sophisticated western examples. There are instruments from the East, as well as local Norwegian work.

The latter includes a massive and ancient organ with scores of rough wooden pipes (the wind supplied by bellows that our guide worked via great vertical leaps), and a series of sweet-sounding green-glass bells with wooden clappers, designed to be hung in the open for the breeze to sound.

After a fashion we sampled one other historic building. On that early morning of our return from the north, we motored up the hill on which rests the Kristiansten Festning (fortress) in order to take breakfast with a view. The solid seventeenth-century fortress was, of course, closed (it is open from 4 to 6 pm), but the park below the walls makes a fine vantage point from which to look at the city. We were carrying out our inspection, eating ancient bread and fresh cheese, and feeling dishevelled by contrast with the neat office girls and smart city gentlemen who kept passing on their way down to work, when all of us and a few thousand seagulls were galvanised by the firing of a cannon from the battlements. It happened again, and again, and again and again, twenty-one times.

But Trondheim does not exist to harbour cathedrals and museums and cannon-firing castles for the benefit of the tourists. It is the trading and cultural heart of middle Norway, and a key hub for road, rail and water communications both within Norway and east to Sweden. It is the country's centre of technical education, and has been for a hundred years.

Trondheimsfjord, with its branches and extensions, is another most extensive sheet of inland water. Unlike the Hardanger and Sogn fjords, it is not close-hemmed by inhospitable mountain plateaux. It is broad and from it radiate a number of fertile valleys. To the north is the Namdal valley, leading to arctic Norway, which we were soon to traverse. Eastwards are the Verdal and Stjørdal valleys, leading to Sweden. Southwards the Nid, Gaula and Orkla valleys point towards Oslo and the rich south-east. The fjord itself provides a path to the open sea, and here Trondheim is a rival to Bergen, though its latitude puts it at a disadvantage with that city.

There are both rail and road links to Sweden, which is less than

a two-hour drive up the Stjørdal valley (the first road to Sweden
was opened in 1835, and the railway in 1882). Many Swedes living
in the somewhat isolated province of Jamtland cross to Trondheim
for a taste of civilisation, repeating by car or train a journey undertaken since settlers from Sweden first occupied the shores of
Trondheimsfjord in the Bronze Age. And within Norway the
railway lines south to Oslo (two), and north to Fauske and Bodø
are vital to the country's present development, with Trondheim
as their focus.

As the capital of the province of Trøndelag, Trondheim has a
flourishing trade, dominated by the export of timber and wood
products, and by fish, salted and canned. The city is a ship-building
centre, though not on the scale of Oslo. Farming is important:
mostly dairy farming, with barley, potatoes, swedes and turnips
for the main crops. Short summers and early frosts make the
growing of wheat risky. I have mentioned the fruit. Driving around
Trøndelag you see farmhouses and barns of a size and number that
exceed those of any district in western Norway. Inland, forestry
dominates the eastern valleys.

All of this is possible because the climatic and geological conditions are relatively favourable. Trondheim lies well inland on its
wide ice-free fjord, protected from the Atlantic winds by a barrier
of gneiss uplands mostly above 1,500ft, yet still warmed by the
Gulf Stream. There are tracts of rich soils bordering the fjord;
most land below the 600ft level is composed of productive sands,
clays and marine deposits laid down in the post-glacial seas before
the land rose to its present height.

5 North to Bodø

The view from the terrace outside the entrance gateway was superb, worth every yard of the steep, slow, rough drive up the mountain. There were two benches at the edge of the drop, one occupied by a trail of ants, the other vacant. We sat drinking coffee and gazing 1,000ft down into the Stjørdal valley, and northwards over forested hills. We had come looking for ancient rock carvings, following the sign that signifies 'a place of interest'; and we had stumbled upon a ruined fortress, Hegra Festning.

The fortress was filled with that melancholy fascination that often invests abandoned human habitation. There were at least five central chambers hollowed out of rock, dripping water and ice-cold by contrast with the warm evening air. Round the perimeter was a rock-carved trench with rifle posts and gun ports; beyond the trench a steep drop and rusting barbed wire. There were signs of violent damage, and there was much natural decay. Yet the surface of the fort was a hill covered with a healing growth of bushes, grass and flowers. At the entrance a memorial tablet told us that here in 1940 six men had died.

At the time we did not find out much more. Later I read of the month-long defence of this old fort, built in 1907 to guard against attack from Sweden, and designed for a garrison of 2,000. With Major Holtermann, the defending commander, were 190 men and a nursing sister, casually assembled after the first surprise German occupation of Trondheim. The Germans attacked and were beaten back, suffered casualties, tied up troops and expended stores that might have been of greater value elsewhere. Within the fort, ammunition, water and food ran short. Some of the men, confined to those dank rock chambers, developed pneumonia. But the fort held until the general surrender in these parts, and became a symbol for the Norwegian resistance. Major Holtermann escaped to Britain.

During our visit the only other people on this wooded mountain were a New Zealand couple in a Land Rover, and an American to whom they were giving a lift. They were on a slow descent from the North Cape (having come up through Sweden) and taught us how to distinguish blueberries from the other black and blue-black berries that abounded. The fortress and the land around it grew not only blueberries but wild strawberries and raspberries. The New Zealanders intended to make blueberry jam. We had strawberries for supper, and gazed through our windows at a beautiful sunset.

We found the rock carvings next morning, down on the other side of the valley near the village of Hegra. There is a sign HELLERISTNINGER pointing off the E75 along a track to the north. After a few hundred yards there is a small grass car-park. From this a short path leads through bushes and steeply up to a convex slab of grey rock, perhaps 10 yards high by 6 yards broad, surrounded by trees, and at a steep angle. The incised carvings had been freshly traced in red paint. At first glance they looked like the doodles of a child (*plate 31*).

Our guidebook calls this 'one of the largest rock-carving sites in Norway' and dates it to c 500 BC. I have not found any other specific reference to it. Nordic rock carvings present complicated problems of dating, and of interpretation on stylistic and cultural grounds. Those who want to study the problems in detail may consult Anders Hagen's book listed in the bibliography.

Briefly, these Hegra carvings belong to the southern Scandinavian or farmers' culture, one of the two broad groups into which the rock carvings are classified. The other is the arctic or hunters' art. Geographically the two groups overlap, and it seems as if they also overlapped in time, though broadly the hunters' art began earlier and probably died out before that of the farmers'. In Scandinavia there is no sharp division between Stone Age and Bronze Age: in many areas the two types of culture probably existed simultaneously

—farming in the valleys, hunting in the mountains and by the sea. In Trøndelag especially, carvings from the two groups occur close to each other, and even on the same rock face, and it is not surprising therefore if there are also overlaps and similarities in the style and subject-matter of the carvings.

The Hegra carvings are very extraordinary, and if they are the first of their kind that you have seen, as in our case, they make a lasting impression. There are so many of them, and the subjects depicted are so curious. There are rows of people, simplified, solid figures, at least one with phallus erect. There are stylised boats, and a few stylised animals, none with antlers (thus none are elk or reindeer, common in the hunters' art). There are plain circles, and circles with a cross or spoke inside (? the sun), outlines of footprints, dots, spirals, swastikas, a pattern like a comb, and other abstract designs that seem impossible to interpret and that imply a developed and complex symbolism. All these are typical of the farmers' carvings.

The hunters' carvings seldom show the human figure, or boats, or domestic animals. They do use geometric or abstract designs. But most often they depict game (elk, reindeer, red deer, bear, fish) with a skilled and beautiful realism (*plate 32*).

It is firmly stated by most experts that rock art 'is a ritual, a magic form of art' (Hagen, 110) devised to increase human fertility, or the stock of game, or sunshine, and that it cannot be simply a means of self-expression for the carver. It is closer to the spirit that created the medieval cathedrals than to a Rodin or a Van Gogh. Modern parallels among the Eskimoes, the Australian aborigines, the South African bushmen, always have a religious motive. And it is likely, though not certain, that at Hegra, and wherever there are carvings in bulk, they were done over a long period and by more than one hand.

Norway has many hundred examples of rock carving and certainly there are more to be discovered. Almost all are in the open, unlike the older rock art of southern Europe. Some are difficult to see, being on steep cliff faces above water. But plenty are accessible if you have the patience to search them out. They bear witness in a particularly direct way to men and women who lived their lives in a hard and dangerous world. What did they think, those carvers of 2,500 years ago, as they tapped and hammered their designs, squatting or kneeling or sitting on this sloping rock, perhaps on a warm, sunny summer morning such as this? No one will ever know and you are as free to speculate as the most expert archaeologist.

We had left our mountain billet so early that it was still only 8 am when we stopped short of the E6 to look at Værnes church, best known for the wooden heads, animal and human, carved at the base of the rafters inside the nave. Værnes houses Trondheim's airport, a distinction of tarnished value. The church was closed. The outside is attractive. It has a tall, square, white-painted stone tower with a copper roof and spire, very simple, almost severe. On the south side is a doorway, the grey stone arch and jambs left unpainted, with a fine carved lion to one side. Værnes church is among the earliest of Norway's stone churches, probably twelfth century.

We had breakfast outside another early church at Alstadhaug, again a stone building painted white. It was in a superb situation, on an isthmus between Trondheimsfjord and a lake, Eidsbotn. In the churchyard is a mound. It looks as though it ought to be old and full of the bones of viking chieftains, but perhaps it is the 'folly' of a nineteenth-century timber exporter. The church was open! Inside are plain round arches of whitened stone, a rococo pulpit of 1626 elaborately carved and painted, and traces of a medieval fresco on the chancel arch.

Next we drove to yet a third church at Stiklestad, where by tradition was fought the battle in which St Olav was killed (page 58). If it seems to the reader that we sometimes overdid the churches, I can only repeat that they are nearly always interesting and beautiful, and that we skipped dozens. Stiklestad is 2 miles east of Verdalsøra. Near the church is a desert of a car park in which three or four buses were scarcely noticeable. Their passengers wandered aimlessly. The church was shut and the *turist inform* was unable to inform. It is a dull spot, and only national piety or extreme tourist conscientiousness need take you there. (The church, of course, may be of interest inside.)

We then spent a frustrating half-hour failing to locate burial mounds at Eggehvammen, just west of Steinkjer. We quartered the area, but saw no mounds or signposts to them. I wanted to inspect at least one genuine mound; but visitors with a similar itch should be warned that mounds are never conspicuous, never signposted, and must mostly be figments of the overheated imaginations of guide-book writers. All the same, this was a well-populated area in the early days. At Bardal, a few miles west—so we learned later and too late—there are rock carvings.

It was soon after this that we picked up a clutch of hitch-hikers. They caught us on the rebound, frustrated by closed churches and skulking mounds. For some days we had ignored them, for in a curious way they rule the roost. Once they are aboard, it is difficult psychologically to stop on impulse, to diverge from the route, to do anything that will delay the progress of one's passengers. Conversation and food have to be shared, which limits both. And the odds on good conversation, the only likely benefit, are less than even. But the E6 was thick with bodies waiting hopefully, and there was a good deal of space in our van.

First we lifted a lone American girl for the length of Lake Snåsa, 27 miles. Lone women on the road are rare, and one imagines pistols and pepper in their handbags. This one had hitch-hiked through sixteen countries. She had a grandmother in Hastings (England) to whom she returned at intervals in order to wash.

Overlapping with our American we took on Gaynor and Dave, a young English couple from Manchester. (Some hitchers carry flags, but as a rule before stopping there is no certainty about national-ities.) They were aiming for Fauske, beyond the Arctic Circle, from where they meant to walk east over the mountains into Sweden.

The drive along Lake Snåsa was beautiful. At the far end we stopped for lunch, sitting on a log by the water's edge, then paddling.

Page 71   13   *Svolvær, capital of Lofoten (page 95). The rock peak is the Svolvær 'Goat', which from below is seen to emerge from the flanks of a higher mountain*

Page 72   (above) 14 *Svolvær, showing the port's complication of inlets and also the strandflat that edges Lofoten's sharp mountains (page 95); (below) 15 fish-drying frames on Lofoten (page 98), empty in summer, but in spring supporting enormous numbers of* stokkfisk

The lake was choppy, little waves breaking on flat stones, and the water receding into a misty distance. It was hot. From here the lone American, with a rucksack that must have weighed 60lb, tramped east towards the village of Snåsa, where there is a youth hostel. The rest of us settled to covering distance northwards, for we wanted time in Lofoten, and our guests wanted time to walk.

After Grong the E6 follows the long Namdalen for some 60 miles. Roughly at the border between North Trøndelag and Nordland it crosses a watershed and begins an equal stretch to Mosjøen. From Steinkjer to Mosjøen there is no sight of the sea, though there is always water somewhere near, and the sea is seldom far. In fact from Trondheim to Tromsø, well north of Narvik, Norway consists of a very narrow indented strip of territory between the mountainous border with Sweden and the Norwegian Sea. This strip is rarely more than 50 miles wide, and at its narrowest is reduced to 4 miles.

Driving north up Namdalen and down the Svenningdal you do not see much of the structure of the country. The two valleys are broad, wooded, with occasional lakes and edged by mountains, lonely, attractive but not riveting. Soon after Majavatn, close to the highest point on this stretch—1,230ft at Lake Sefri—we stopped for the night, driving north-east up a side road to camp on a hillside in Fiplingdalen, somewhere beyond Kvanni. We had done 215 miles since leaving Hegra at six (except for short stretches, all on tarmac), had made numerous stops, and were tired.

On the other side of our valley was a high ridge, the edge of Børgefjellet and the Børgefjell National Park, wild empty country stretching to the Swedish border 25 miles off. The ridge still held some snow. As always, it pays to gain a little height, for we were now in a magnificent setting.

I walked down into the valley to wash. On a trip such as ours there is much to frustrate cleanliness. Here mosquitoes discouraged more than a lightning exposure of bare skin. But where I met the stream it ran over an extraordinary rock formation, striated black and white in bands about two inches broad, shining under the clear

E

water. And downstream the water disappeared into a hole. I explored for some way towards the upper Fipling lake, avoided more holes among the bushes, but saw no more water.

Gaynor and Dave had a small orange tent which they set up in a clearing of sorts a few yards off the road. They lit a fire, cooked on a primus, and in every way behaved, had to behave, more like true travellers than we, with our house on wheels and our portable gaz. Only one car passed that whole evening, but after supper we became islanded by cows and bullocks on whose evening forage trail we had parked. Round about were large patches of willow herb and a field of meadow sweet. The land here had mostly been cleared of forest, secondary growth was scarcely begun, and the flower armies had invaded magnificently.

That night the mosquitoes found our open sky-light and at intervals dive-bombed. At 5.30 it began to rain, which also woke me. Thus we set off again early. The tent was soaked, the back of the van was choked with rucksacks and boots caked in red mud, and clouds covered the hill tops.

This day, 2 August, we covered 231 miles and stopped just short of Fauske. There is not a lot to be said about the drive for we did little sightseeing. Mosjøen is at the head of a fjord; it exports timber and produces aluminium from a plant opened in 1958. We did not even inspect 'the oldest octagonal church in north Norway', and sternly rejected the temptations of the many side roads east and west that litter the map here and for the next stretch to Mo i Rana. Mo is a considerable town. We stopped there on the return, and also carried through a diversion or two in the area, so it will be best to leave it until then (page 105).

The one object that I had determined to see behaved to us as had the burial mounds at Eggehvammen. Not far beyond Mo, at Reinforshei, is what one of our books described as the longest salmon ladder in Europe. I had not even seen a short salmon ladder. We quartered the area back and forth, tried for directions from a garage girl who spoke no English, and generally became frustrated. A new road was being driven through just here, and we assumed that the way to the ladder had been temporarily obliterated. On the return journey I enquired about the ladder at the tourist information office in Mo. 'Oh, you cannot *see* it. It is in a tunnel. We often are asked about that.'

The road to the Arctic Circle from Mo leads up the Dunderland valley, mostly with a good surface. The Dunderlandsdalen is a fine wide valley with forested flanks and snow-patched rock peaks and ridges rising to 4,000ft on either side. Again, it would pay to gain height by diverting up a side road, as we did on our return. The Rana river runs deep in the centre, green and swift. The railway flits in and out of tunnels, mostly on the other bank. There are occasional farms. They are dairy farms, with hay for winter feed almost the only crop. At Storvollen, river, road and rail turn a right-angle to south of east for a few miles, the valley narrows and the sides steepen. Beyond Krokstrand all three turn north once more, and here begin to climb to the Saltfjell and the Arctic Circle.

It is a most fortunate accident for the romantics of the world that the E6, the Arctic Highway, the only motorable road in Norway that crosses the Arctic Circle, crosses it at 2,130ft near the top of a barren plateau. A few miles north or south and the magic point would have been cosily tucked into some deep valley, a tame business. Just here, at 66° 32′ N, there are no such valleys for the road and rail to follow. The Saltfjell (*fjell* = mountain) stretches east to the Swedish border only 6 miles off, and westward lies the ice-capped mass of the Svartisen, with glaciers reaching almost to the sea. The treeless, rock-strewn moorland slopes, with snow still lying on the northern ridges, and an enormous sky, are a fit setting. Here is perhaps the true division between south and north. And for us, after a dull morning, the sun came out.

The Circle is marked at the roadside by a stone monument dated 1937, the year when this section of the Highway was opened. That was a great achievement. Close by is a café full of souvenirs, generally crowded, with a post office that offers a Polar Circle stamp and postmark. But walk 300 yards along the road or up the hill and the hut is dwarfed by the size of the country; the figures and

the parked cars no longer matter, and even the railway farther down
the slope, with its protecting pattern of windbreaks and wooden
tunnels, merges into the landscape. The railway is kept open
throughout the winter with the aid of rotary snow-ploughs. The
road is still sometimes overwhelmed.

Soon after Stødi the Highway begins the fairly gentle descent of
the Lønsdalen, and is back among the silver birch. This is a lovely
drive on a good surface and should not be hurried. The river swirls
and tumbles along its rock base, the trees get thicker, taller and more
varied, the valley deeper, narrower, and there are many places that
invite one to take a break. Soon one is again among farms and
forestry plantations, and the valley becomes the Saltdalen and leads
to Rognan at the head of the Saltdalsfjord. Rognan has been a boat-
building centre probably since viking days.

It was time to camp. From the map we picked a short track that
leads east beyond Rognan and beside Lake Botn. It was the lake that
attracted us, but in fact it was not possible to get the van close, for
the track runs high above the lake to a private holiday settlement of
some kind at the far end. But it is a very beautiful lake, cupped by
steep rock faces rising hundreds of feet.

We spent the night on the edge of a war cemetery. Here at Botn
are buried 1,657 Yugoslavs, 2,732 Germans and some Russians.
The Yugoslavs, so far from home, were part of a consignment of
8,000 transported to North Norway by the Germans during World
War II. They were set to work on improving the Arctic Highway.
Less than 1,000 survived and few of the names of their dead are
recorded. In a separate enclosure the Germans are nearly all named,
on hundreds of small plaques let into the earth. At the far end of their
cemetery the dead from the *Scharnhorst* are commemorated. The
Russians have a single stone memorial.

The stretch of road between Botn and Fauske is among the most
beautiful of the entire route from Trondheim to Narvik. It follows
the Saltdalsfjord, along the shore or high above it. There was a

pearly light on the water, and a backdrop of mountains-with-snow indistinct in the morning haze. Out on the water there was one man in an orange life-jacket standing in a small boat. He and the boat and the water were so still that they might have been from a painting. The railway was below the road, in and out of tunnels, mostly in. The road too required one long tunnel, half a mile of it; there was no other car as we went through and going north a curve at the far end cuts off any view of daylight. Lighted bands of rough-hewn rock alternate with shadow, the entrance behind grows smaller and smaller, the lights stretch ahead for ever. It is a modern entry point for Hades.

Gaynor and Dave disembarked at Fauske. They intended next day to take the train east to the copper-mine town of Sulitjelma and from there to cross the Sulitjelma mountains into Sweden. The Sulitjelma is the highest range in North Norway, over 6,000ft, with glaciers and permanent snow. We had a letter from them afterwards. They had enjoyed a fine seven-day trek despite finding that the railway to Sulitjelma was being converted to a road, and was at that moment neither one nor the other.

At Fauske somewhere there are supposed to be quays made of marble from a neighbouring quarry. This improbable fact leads one by association to imagine Italian gardens, piazzas and orgies. But the only quay we stepped upon was made of wood, and Fauske is a very ordinary little modern town. From it the North Norway Bus starts its regular scheduled run to Kirkenes, by the Russian border. There are three overnight stops. For travellers without cars, a train ticket from Oslo to Fauske, and a bus ticket on, would provide a fairly painless way of experiencing the length of the country.

We obtained from the information office a tide timetable for the Saltstraumen Eddy. The Eddy is a maelstrom. It is 36 miles from Fauske west along route 80 (mostly tar) towards Bodø, and then south, a lovely drive, to the end of route 813 (a dirt road). Four times a day 80,000 million gallons of water (how on earth is this calculated?) sweep in or out of a narrow strait that links the inland expanse of Skjerstadfjord with the Saltfjord and the open sea, the

intercepting shallows being a glacial moraine. The maelstrom is most
spectacular on the days of the spring tides, and in any case should be
seen when the current is at its strongest. Hence the need for a
timetable.

We aimed at an 11.15 outgoing tide and just made it. Although
the moon was not full for another week, the water was still impressive, racing, swirling, with white whirlpools erupting like sub-
terranean explosions, and a roaring noise as from a large waterfall.
There were hundreds of gulls and terns diving for the fish that were
being swept out. Anglers shared this harvest. We sat on the low
rock cliffs for a long time, absorbed.

There are jagged mountains across the strait to the south. One
day I mean to take the ferry from Vågan (on route 80) across to
Skjerstad. From there route 812, with several branches, leads into
this mountain country, the area bounded by the E6 to the east,
Skjerstadfjord to the north, the Svartisen massif to the south, and the
island-studded sea. The island fringe can be visited, according to the
Bodø guide, by a combination of route 810 and ferries, starting from
Bodø and finishing at Nesna, from where route 805 returns to Mo.
This coastline south of Bodø is said to be some of the finest. Another
way inland is to branch off the E6 up the mountain road from Medby
in the Saltdal valley. I place this territory high on my list of priorities.

In fact Bodø, the Nordland capital, to which we made our way
after leaving Saltstraumen, is a town that would make a very
satisfactory base for an entire holiday. The average temperatures in
July and August are 13.6° and 12.7°C (Bergen, 15.0° and 14.7°;
Oslo, 17.3° and 15.9°), which is warmer than might be expected.
For ornithologists, walkers, climbers, fishermen, and for lovers of
pottering in marvellous scenery, the area must be hard to surpass.
It is from Bodø rather than from Lofoten, for example, that it seems
easiest to arrange boat trips to the bird-rich island groups of Værøy
(4 million birds) and Røst (1½ million birds). There are regular
steamer services to Narvik and to Lofoten, though a car ferry for the
latter means driving north to Skutvik (see page 83). At Bodø the
midnight sun is visible, clouds permitting, from 1 June to 12 July.

And for total darkness try the period from 19 December to 9 January.

Bodø was destroyed by bombs in May 1940 during the closing stages of the Norwegian campaign. It was being used as a base by the British. So the present town is new, though its history as a settlement dates from 1803, and its charter from 1816. The idea was to give the north a town that would release it from economic dependence on Bergen and Trondheim. In this Bodø was never fully successful. Yet to the casual visitor it now appears to flourish. One reason for this must be its recent importance as a communication centre. Since 1962 it has been the northern terminus of the Nordland Railway, and looks like remaining so. We ourselves had just travelled the road route, completed in 1940, which presents no difficulties. There is an all-weather airfield (and NATO airbase) and of course a well-developed shipping port.

I say all this in favour of the town despite the fact that throughout our visit it drizzled. Perhaps we liked it because Mary met two small English-speaking boys who for one krone a head, and with the aid of a penknife, were letting the ladies in and out through the jammed door of a washroom in a café. They abandoned this piece of private enterprise for another, and led us to the fishing-boat harbour, took us down to one boat amongst the scores moored there, and negotiated for us a purchase for Kr2.50 (very cheap) of some fine-looking fish of unknown breed from a box on the deck. Up on the quayside we bought fresh shrimps cheaper than we ever got them again.

Do not miss the cathedral, completed in 1956, open in summer from 12 to 3 pm. It is a winner. The outside is plain, almost traditional—reinforced concrete walls rising in three stages, narrow windows, copper-roofed, and a separate and beautiful bell-tower. The inside is rich in form, colour and detail. The walls arch inward three times in quarter circles, eventually to meet high overhead. An absence of columns gives this design a feeling of immense space. The woodwork is a warm red-brown. There is strong but delicate stained glass at both ends. On the lowest level of wall hang ten large rugs, designed and made by one local woman, of symbolic design

and soft, merging colours. The organ and its pipes have been
designed into the west end, forming a frame for a rose window.
There is much to examine that cannot be mentioned here. And
nearby is a museum, which we did not sample.

It was still raining when we stopped a mile east of Vågan on the
return drive to Fauske to search for 'a magnificent rock-carving of
an elk, some 4,000 years old'. In company with a Norwegian boy
from another car (whose adult inhabitants wisely stayed put) we
climbed for half a mile up a very wet peaty path through heather,
between birch trees (which at this latitude seem to be full grown at
20–30ft), and across a stream to an enormous slab of sloping rock
where the path stopped. By now it was raining hard. We clambered
around with umbrellas aloft and soaking from the knees down. At
last from a position high on the side of the rock two ears, a muzzle
and part of a body were revealed. There were many other natural
marks on the rock, which was streaming with water, and it was
clear why such carvings can lie so long 'undiscovered' by modern
man. A coating of moss or lichen, a little flaking from a few
thousand frosts, the growth of bushes, trees and grass in the cracks
of a rock—or simply an absence of observers as the evening light
casts the long shadows best for such discoveries—and a carving
remains most efficiently camouflaged.

It was still raining as we ate our shrimps and dried out in a lay-by
beside the Valnesfjord, and still raining as we drove north out of
Fauske at 6.30 that evening. I thought that it would be good to
place the Sommarset-Bonnåsjøen ferry behind us before sleeping,
and it proved easy to do so. Once across the Fauskeidet, a kind of
wide marsh, the road is one of the most recent sections completed
(1966), with a fine wide asphalt surface. We reached Sommarset in
an exciting twenty minutes, through six tunnels and across two high
bridges. Between the tunnels, with their walls of jagged rock and
their mesmerising diminuendi of lights, there were blinding views
across the waters of the fjords to mountains beheaded by cloud and
hazed by rain. One tunnel curves through a rock spur and straight
on to the Trengsel bridge. The sixth tunnel, the Kalvik, of nearly

3,000 yards, is the longest on the E6. This whole section replaces a fifty-minute ferry journey that used to take off from Røsvik on the western side of Sørfolda. The new ferry takes fifteen minutes.

It was still raining when, a few miles beyond Bonnåsjøen, up on a pass beneath the smooth granite sweep of Blåfjellet (3,287ft) we came to an expanse of level gravel that enabled us to get a little distance from the road. Between us and Blåfjellet were 300 yards of low trees and heather. We could only sense the top; the rock slid up and up and mysteriously into shifting cloud. Another great mountain loomed on the other side of the road. The Bodø fish were delicious.

6 To Narvik

There was heavy rain through the night, and rain heavy or light for all of the 115 miles to Narvik. In such weather it is good not to be in a tent, not to be disputing with wet canvas, unable to move house without a soaking. Our motorcaravan was dry, it was warm; we could cook, sleep, read and write in comfort, and in seconds we could lower the roof and drive away.

Yet the rain was sad for I had been much looking forward to this section of the road, which 'gives a wonderful cross-section of the weird and sagalike beauty of Nordland country' (*Tourist in Norway*, 117). I am not certain what to expect of beauty that is 'sagalike', but on this journey we were not allowed to discover. Water streamed in continuous sheets down the numerous and vast rock slopes, the rivers were in spate, and only the bottom halves of the mountains were on view. Clouds hung in shifting masses, revealing, then concealing, rock and waterfall. The road itself was often awash. Water poured down every runnel and filled every hole.

On one desolate hillside we passed a solitary roadman. He was digging shallow channels diagonally across the road to help drain it. I think of him sometimes: it is always raining, and he is moving slowly up and down the hills and the hairpin bends; his digging is not of the slightest use, and he knows it, but it is something he must do, because that is his fate.

This road from Bonnåsjøen ferry to within a few miles of Narvik was the worst we had encountered, a real bone-shaker that exhausted us and was unkind to the van. The holes were filled with water; there was no distinguishing the shallow from the deep. We moved at below 30 mph for most of the time, but were overtaken all day by drivers pushing at the 50 mph limit, aquaplaning along the highway like speedboats.

A non-asphalted section of the Arctic Highway can vary greatly, from week to week, from day to day. In summer beneath the heavy traffic it can deteriorate quickly. On this journey north we met just about the worst conditions. Returning less than a week later we found the road had been regraded, was dry, and gave a very reasonable drive.

Apart from rain and cloud, my chief memory of this stretch is of lakes. There were dozens of them, filling every hollow in the valleys like the rain had filled the hollows of the road. Descending towards the Sagfjord there is a succession of seven lakes. Some have patches of sandy shoreline; all have islands and peninsulas dotted with fishing huts.

Between the last lake and the head of the fjord is a short stretch of turbulent river that has worn for itself a narrow canyon through its rock bed. At the upper end of this stretch, on a section of rock wall on the opposite side of the river from the main road, are carvings of two beautiful browsing reindeer in the naturalistic hunters' style. There is no paint to identify them, but the moss has been removed and they are easily seen, even in the rain. Estimates of the age of these reindeer vary from 8,000 to 5,000 years old. A track leaves the road westwards at this point, and the carvings are just downstream of a wooden bridge that takes the track across the river. Incidentally, it is worth following the river as far as another wooden bridge at the lower end, for the swirling falls and the great slabs of smooth grey rock that confine them are impressive.

At Ulsvåg, route 81 goes west to Skutvik (23 miles) and the ferry to Lofoten (see page 101), while the E6 makes for Bognes and the ferry to Skarberget, 5 miles and half an hour across Tysfjorden. From Bognes there is also a ferry to Lødingen across the Vestfjord (1½ hours) from where you can join route 19 and reach both Harstad, capital of the Vesterålen islands, and Lofoten, without the bother of driving the land route via Narvik. It saves about 150 miles, but you would miss some splendid country.

The ferry crossing to Skarberget is said to be the finest on the E6, with mountains rising from the sea in every direction. For us there was rain and low cloud. When we stopped for lunch on the next pass at 800ft the view was all cloud and we never left the van. At Saetran, three bridges, some five new miles of highway and a tunnel have, since 1969, replaced the old ferry-crossing of the narrow Efjorden. The bridges, of varying construction, span the gaps between two islands. The clouds lifted a little here and disclosed a mysterious and very beautiful view up the fjord, as delicate and stylised as a Chinese painting: low wooded peninsulas fingering into the water, and beyond them misty mountains, layer after layer receding into clouds.

For the last 25 miles the road skirts the wide Ofotfjord and shows increasing evidence of human activity. There might have been a new bridge for us at Skjomenfjord, for the books gave 1972 as the opening date. The bridge was there and looked fine and ready, but it was the ferry that took us over. Perhaps they were awaiting the arrival of a king or a ski champion or Miss Norway 1971 to open it. Or perhaps the foreman had gone walkabout before tightening the last six bolts.

And so to Narvik.

Narvik is an undistinguished, even ugly, town in a most beautiful setting. To appreciate the setting fully you need height, and the quickest way to achieve this is to take the *telecabine* 2,000ft up Mount Fagernesfjell. Beside the top station is a restaurant with both open and enclosed viewing points. The view is fantastic, for Narvik is on a peninsula surrounded by fjords, and the fjords are enclosed by mountains. Even from the restaurant platform there is an un- restricted arc of some 200° to inspect: blue water, blue mountains, white clouds in a blue sky, that is what was laid at our feet next morning, for the bad weather had lifted and a bright sun shone.

One writer says that 'this view is at its most magnificent in winter when the arctic sun reflects off the snow and the silvery waters of the fjord' (Douglas, 103). Fagernesfjell has ski-jumps, a slalom hill and downhill ski runs. Also it would be a fine place from which to watch the midnight sun (26 May to 19 July). By climbing higher—for there are more mountains above the restaurant—the mountains to the east and south-east can be seen, peaks that rise to over 6,000ft in the Storsteinfjell and hold permanent ice fields.

The population of Narvik is about 16,000. Its official foundation was in 1901 and the reason for its existence smites the eyes of anyone who stops to shop in Kongensgate, the main street; for the Swedish LKAB works dominate the centre, with a great conveyor apparatus striding over streets and buildings, and loading quays (the Malmkai) just where a town esplanade should be. Narvik was created to export Swedish iron ore mined in the hills round Kiruna. From the head of Rombaksbotn, north of Narvik, to the Swedish border is only 5 miles. Sweden's own ports on the Gulf of Bothnia are closed by ice for six months of the year, while Narvik is not. So between 1883 and 1902 a railway was built, the Ofot line, with a present capacity for carrying 15 million tons of ore annually. Narvik's port installations are claimed to be the most modern in the world. And all this lies at your feet, as on a map, from the Fagernesfjell platform.

The Ofot line (the Swedish section is called the Lapland Railway) runs a passenger service. A trip to Abisko and Kiruna (and on, if you wish, to Lulea on the Gulf of Bothnia, and to Stockholm) is said to be rewarding. In two hours (59 miles) you are transported from fjord country into Arctic tundra, and Abisko is a base for excursions into the Lapland mountains, while at Kiruna a tour round the huge iron mines can be arranged.

For the British, Narvik is, or was, famous for the naval battles of World War II, when two destroyer actions were fought in the harbour and surrounding fjords. The town was occupied by the Germans in a daring operation on 9 April 1940, was recaptured on 28 May by Norwegian forces, assisted by French and Polish troops. It was evacuated within a few days because the German invasion of France required that all Allied strength, particularly naval, be concentrated close to the main threat. It seems now to be agreed that

Narvik could have been retaken by the Allies far earlier, with less loss of life and greater effect on morale, if the commander of the British Brigade, which landed at Harstad in early April, had been less cautious. Contrary to my own expectations, I could find very few British graves in the war cemetery; they were mostly of men from the navy and the RAF.

Near the centre of the town in the market place there is a small war museum displaying photographs, maps, newspaper cuttings, models and samples of weapons, uniforms, etc. The photos are interesting: amongst other things they show how much of central Narvik was destroyed. The Germans came to Narvik to safeguard the iron ore; the British came to deny the ore to the Germans. Thus iron ore created Narvik, destroyed it, and has now recreated it.

In Narvik we saw another beautiful rock carving of a reindeer. It is on a sloping slab of rock facing out to sea above the *Småbåthavn* (small-boat harbour). It can be reached by finding the suburban road called Bjørkveien, near the pretty Guldbransons Park. From this leads a road called Einerveien from whose dead-end a path winds down through bushes to the carving (*Helleristninger* on the town map). The carving is in the naturalistic style, simple, like a quick sketch by Picasso (*plate 32*). And Einerveien will display for you examples of recent small town houses, Norwegian style, mostly of wood, many with gay gardens.

The camp site at Narvik is on a sloping field down by the fjord on the northern edge of the town. We parked the van close to the beach and could look straight across water to the beautiful hills of Skånland. But whenever I view my slide of the camp I remember even more vividly the bus-load of formidable Finnish ladies who drove up early in the morning, debussed, and set about producing breakfast for themselves with Japanese discipline. They took over the camp, or rather the cookhouse, the ladies' washroom and a large open space near by. It was unexpected and a little frightening. They boiled water in a kettle so large it would have roused the envy of any of the Norwegian giants who no doubt still survive in the more secluded strongholds of the mountains.

The showers in the men's washroom, whose sanctity the Finnish ladies respected, provided a new permutation of the obstacles to cleanliness. The water was warm, but to prevent excessive use one had to hang on to a chain to provoke a flow. Then one had to let go so as to soap oneself. Then there was no water. And so on.

At Narvik the Arctic Highway is merely getting into its stride. There are another 647 miles to Kirkenes on the Russian border. Look at it on a large-scale map, snaking over tundra plateaux and down to bleak fjords. It entices, like Odysseus's sirens. The roads one does not travel always remain an ache in the head. Yet the road we did travel was remarkable. I believe it would be difficult to find a route more beautiful for every mile of its way than route 19, through Hinnøya, the Vesterålen islands and Lofoten. Though we regretted the need to choose between Lofoten and the farther north, we did not regret our choice.

But first the Highway itself gave us one last thrill. Guiltily ignoring the groups of hitch-hikers—for the call of the North Cape to the young of Europe is as strong as the spring call that sends the birds from Africa to the Arctic—we soon reached the suspension bridge (a toll bridge) over the mouth of the Rombaksbotn. This was completed in 1964, the largest suspension bridge in Norway, with a total span of 2,500ft, and the roadway 150ft above the water. It is beautiful to look at and beautiful to look from.

7 Vesterålen and Lofoten

It is at Bjerkvik just beyond the Rombak bridge that route 19 leaves the Arctic Highway. For us it was a perfect afternoon, sunny, not too hot, with plenty of photogenic white cloud. Most of the first 90 miles is recent asphalt, not yet on the maps. This was a blessed relief after the jolting of the previous day. We did not hurry. At lunch I bathed, a first (and last) bathe above the Arctic Circle, cool but not cold. That was from a beach layered with superb polishable stones.

Where the land allows, where it is not steep mountains, peat, swamp, lake or low birch forest, there are still farms, a surprising number of them—some potatoes, mostly pasture. The hay was being cut and draped on drying wires. This may have been a second crop. In these latitudes, with near-perpetual day in the summer, so soon as the snow has melted vegetable growth goes into frenzied activity that scarcely pauses through the twenty-four hours until the first frosts. Warmth may be absent for ripening, but light will not go away. It was from the turf roof of one small red-painted barn near Ostervik that we saw three birch trees growing, a record for our trip; one was dead, and one was a tiddler, but one at 10ft was a giant of a roof-birch for 68° 31′ N.

The narrow Tjeldsund separates the mainland from the island of Hinnøy the largest of Norway's islands (except for the dependency of Spitzbergen) and the first of the Vesterålen islands. The channel is crossed by a fine new bridge (toll) that arches spectacularly over the water, rising from low banks to 135ft in the centre. On the far side

Page 89 (above) 16 *Røros, with the eighteenth-century church built from the profits of copper-mining; slag heaps in the foreground* (page 120); (below) 17 *the church at Seljord, Telemark, reputedly twelfth century; typical of the early stone churches put up in the richer districts* (page 162)

Page 90 (left)
18 *interior of a paper-mill, one of the more straightforward uses to which wood is put these days (page 137);*
(below) 19 *a collecting-point for floating logs on the Glomma river at Fetsund (page 136). Logs have been floated down the rivers of Norway for hundreds of years*

route 83 leads north to Harstad (17 miles), an important port and a garrison town. The medieval church of Trondenes is close by. From Harstad it is possible to continue round the north-east part of Hinnøy and, with one ferry, to rejoin route 19 at Langsvassbukt. North of Harstad is the little island of Bjarkøya, prolific of eiderduck and their eiderdown. Eiderdown has been collected for centuries. We did not go to Harstad. We turned south at the bridge and followed down the other side of the Tjelsund, passing through a string of small waterside settlements, each with a group of rowingboats moored near the shore.

We looked for somewhere to camp. It did not prove easy. I wanted a waterside camp, but the few flat patches off the road were always inconsiderately occupied by houses, barns or fields. At length we came to rest just short of Fiskfjord, down a short track leading to an old jetty. We parked by the jetty, masked from the road by a steep grass bank with birch trees at the top.

Round the head of this miniature fjord are steep mountains with the customary decoration of snow in the gulleys. The sun left the jetty early, but did not abandon the high peaks until 9.30 pm. It never grew quite dark. We watched arctic terns fishing a few yards out from our windows. Whenever one was successful, others chased it.

The next day (6 August) brought a superb drive. The weather was perfect, sunshine against great banks of white and grey cloud. The sea was an intense blue, choppy with a breeze. The mountains became increasingly spectacular and were sharp to the most distant horizon.

The Vesterålen islands are all mountainous, with peaks rising commonly to 2,000ft and some above 3,000ft. But, as we were to discover before the end of the day, they tend to own a wider and richer coastal fringe than do the islands of Lofoten. Where we travelled there is an almost continuous chain of farms, with pasture and woods on the lower hill slopes. Indeed, the Vesterålen have some of the best farmland in North Norway, which, together with the rich off-shore fishing, has ensured occupation at least since early viking times.

F

Hinnøy, on which we had spent the night, is most curiously shaped: fjords cut deep into it from many angles. Crossing a pass between the head of one fjord and another we came upon the first and only herd of goats we saw, though from older accounts of Norwegian life they must once have been common (they have declined from 248,916 in 1939 to 82,056 in 1971). We had entered a cirque of mountain peaks, the Vestpolltind, from which there seemed no way out, and advancing slowly up the road was this middle-aged man with some fifty white she-goats. He led them off the road into the shade of a grove of birch, where he sat on the grass, sun-speckled, and talked to them, fondled each in turn of those that clustered round. He should have produced a pipe on which to play mountain music, and no doubt did so after we had gone, for here, somehow brought to life in Arctic Norway, was a painting from an urn of classical Greece. Perhaps these goats, like many others, are owned for the brown cheese that is made from their milk, which we enjoyed but which is not to everyone's liking. It is not strong, has a kind of scented taste, and keeps well.

Waiting for the Strand-Sortland ferry there is a great view across water to the south-west of layers of jagged mountains. This strait or sound between Hinnøy and Langøy is on the route taken by the coastal express on its 2,500-mile voyage from Bergen to Kirkenes and back, a voyage that must be one of the most spectacular anywhere. The better part of it lies in waters sheltered from the open sea by skerries and islands; for from ten to twelve days the boats pass mountains and glaciers, slide through the narrowest of straits, and visit a succession of beautifully situated ports.

The first steamer to sail in North Norway initiated a revolution which it is now hard to appreciate. When ships were dependent on wind, current and reasonable weather, postal and other services were unreliable and very slow. Travel by land was even slower: to journey from Tromsø to Oslo could take months. There was no continuous road system. Much of the north could only be reached by water. Thus the thirteen coastal steamers that in our times run a regular service, summer and winter, night and day, besides providing an unforgettable experience for tourists, perform a continuing task in linking the northern coastal communities with each other and with the rest of Norway. In northern Norway airfields, railways and roads are modern arrivals. The Arctic Highway was not completed until 1941, the railway to Bodø in 1962, and most of the airfields in the last twenty-five years. Road and air travel can still be interrupted by weather.

Sortland existed in viking times. It is now a large village, administrative centre of Vesterålen, and the farthest north we achieved. Keeping to route 19, we drove down the broad littoral of the southeast coast of Langøy along a good dirt road with magnificent views for the entire way.

At lunch above a line of seaweed-covered rocks we found the beach littered with fragments of shell and white coral. They must have travelled with the Gulf Stream across the Atlantic from the Caribbean. Some lumps of coral were the size of golf balls. Since these could not have floated, they are perhaps transported by seaweed, seaweed that was growing from the coral and with it is torn from its home by storms and then slowly pushed east day by day.

From Sandnes there is a ten-minute ferry to Stokmarknes on the island of Hadseløy. The crewman who sold us tickets remarked on how mild were the island winters. And on his advice we took the west-about route round Hadseløy, 16 miles, almost without traffic, and very beautiful.

At one point we walked across fields to a rock promontory much like those of Devon and Cornwall, with tidal pools full of seaweeds, small fish, snails, sea urchins etc, and the rock heavily fissured, easy for scrambling. There were crowds of gulls screeching at the intrusion. Westwards there was nothing but sea between us and Greenland.

The fields included one of potato plants with purple flowers. Potatoes are a staple crop throughout Norway, and purple-flowered plants are common here. In England I have seen only white flowers. There is a curious absence of visible life in these northern farmhouses: no dogs, cats, chickens, children or adults. Farming is only a part-time employment, and the men earn as much or more by fishing. But where are the wives and the smaller children?

Rounding the coast to Melbu and the next of the ferries there are marvellous views of the north-western length of the Lofot wall. Ideally one should circumnavigate Lofoten by boat, for to realise fully their extent, height and savage beauty it is necessary to be at a little distance from them. But if this is impossible, then the view from the south-west shore of Hadseløy should be tried. My friend Mattieu Williams (see bibliography) advises visiting Lofoten at the end of June or early July when still mantled with snow, and when the midnight sun is on display.

About the Lofot 'wall': although Lofoten consist of four large islands (Austvågøy, Vestvågøy, Flakstadøy and Moskenesøy), a few smaller islands, and swarms of islets and skerries, from almost any angle they appear as a continuous narrow jagged chain that for 60 miles runs south-west into the Norwegian Sea, and hence do form a wall that shelters the sea approach up the Vestfjord to Narvik. The mountains commonly rise to between 2,500 and 3,000ft, and in places reach higher. Since the horizontal distance between many of the summits and the sea's edge is often small, the result for the human eye is truly breathtaking. I doubt that the most jaded traveller could fail to be moved by it.

The peculiar savagery of the bare precipices, knife-edge *arêtes*, needle peaks and numerous deep corries or cirques is, of course, the result of glaciation. If in doubt about any strange physical aspect of Norway, you may ascribe it to glaciation with tolerable safety. In this case it is thought that during the last period of the last ice age, ice-fields from the mainland reached to Lofoten but did not submerge them. The islands developed their own glaciers which in descending scraped and gouged off the flesh of the mountains, leaving a kind of skeleton of a range for the frosts and suns of later centuries to work upon. The result is perfectly splendid for painters, photographers and mad rock climbers.

Sailing to Fiskebøl from Melbu (thirty minutes) the boat appears to

be aiming at a bare mountain side. There is no house visible and no
place to land. Eventually two low islands detach themselves from
the mass and a passage between them leads round to a landing-stage
tucked beneath the mountain. There is nothing else.

We took the main road to Svolvær. It is a well-engineered
route (asphalt) through dramatic scenery, for it skirts under mountains and above a narrow fjord on whose other side rises very sharply
the highest peak in Lofoten—Higravstind, 3,800ft. This was not
camping country and we were glad to reach gentler shores near
Svolvær, for it was after 5 pm.

We were chased from our first camp site by a rising tide. The sea
had been some way off beyond a low ridge of rocks, but it approach-
ed unseen through devious channels and suddenly flooded a sandy
flat beside us and about 2ft lower. It was quite disconcerting to look
up from writing notes to see terns fishing where we had so recently
walked. Probably the van was safe, for it was parked on a gravel
track, and an inch or two of sea around the wheels would not have
harmed. But we had not enough faith or placidity of mind. We
should not have slept. So at 8.30 pm, with the sea lapping close, we
left and found a minute private corner above Svolvær, with a lake
behind, one of the town's harbours below, and a long waterfall
connecting the two sounding in our ears.

Svolvær, whose normal population of about 4,000 increases
dramatically during the cod-fishing season, is the capital of Lofoten
and administrative centre of the Lofot fishery. It is built on a flattish
peninsula, part of the strandflat that is such a characteristic feature of
much of the Norwegian west coast. But the sea bites into the
peninsula in so many and such unexpected places that it is not at first
easy to make sense of the geography of the port (*plates 13 & 14*).
Towering behind is the peak of Blåtind (1,958ft).

The strandflat has been defined as that part of the coastal area
lying around 100ft above sea level and about 30ft beneath it.
Occasionally it can be 25 miles wide, but generally it is only a mile

or two. It is a kind of ledge or bench whose origins are still disputed, a rim of more or less horizontal rock on a coast whose characteristic lines are vertical. Much of the visible strandflat consists of those low islands and skerries that separate the mountains from the true ocean. In North Norway especially the strandflat makes it possible for human communities to exist. Without it there would be few farms and the fishing would be very different.

Svolvær is a pleasant little town in a beautiful setting. It is on the coastal express route, has a frequent car ferry service to the mainland at Skutvik, and a fairweather airport, so it is busy, growing, and full of visitors during the summer. Unexpectly it had no *Turist Inform*, and so no free maps or leaflets. Matters of this sort seem to be arranged in far off Bodø, and it was fortunate that I had there obtained, as an afterthought, a good leaflet guide to the islands.

We went down into the town late. Low cloud and pattering rain pushed us into doing accounts and working out travel schedules, for we were now at the apogee of our journey. We had travelled 1,600 miles, used up eighteen days, and it was necessary to take stock of cash and time. I reckoned that the cash would last if we continued to be careful—being careful meant that sitting in an upstairs café on Svolvær's main square to a coffee and cake apiece was quite an event —and that we could potter in Lofoten for three or four days.

So in uncertain weather but good heart we drove the few miles south to Kabelvåg—the oldest fishing port in Lofoten with a history from viking times—to look at the Lofot Museum and Aquarium. The building that houses both is not easy to find, being at the end of a road that twists between houses that line several small arms of the harbour. It turns out to be a *rorbu*, a fisherman's house, nestling behind a stout breakwater, with the open sea beyond. It has two rooms, the upper devoted to the Lofot fishing industry, the lower to the aquarium.

The aquarium displays many local fish, both freshwater and salt, and beasts such as crabs, sea urchins, starfish and eels. The museum contains a lot of photographs (a few with English captions) of the fishing fleets of former years, of fishermen and fisherwives, of drying the catch on rock and wooden frames. There are models of the boats, and collections of nets, floats, weights, hooks, and much else recalling the toughness and the skills of a traditional way of life which goes back hundreds of years and which even today underpins the prosperity, directly or indirectly, of thousands.

The great Lofot fishery still takes place every year. Although the boats no longer rely on oar and sail, and although refrigeration and powered winches, nylon, echo-sounding apparatus and other technical developments of material and method have to some extent changed the scene, some things have altered little. The shoals of Arctic cod still enter the Vestfjord (which is 100 miles wide at its mouth) from the Barents Sea to spawn about the end of January. They are still fished from then until mid April. During this period the population of some Lofot villages increases tenfold. The increase used to be greater, but the number of fish and of fishermen is down by more than half.

At this time snow mantles the mountains down to the sea; and the harbours, so comparatively empty of boats and people when seen by the summer visitor, are each night crowded with masts and oilskins. By day the Vestfjord is a swarm of little ships, for the small boat with an individual owner still predominates. All this can be seen from the museum photographs.

Although cod no longer forms the great bulk of the Norwegian catch of fish as once it did (cod, it will be recalled, brought the Hansa to Bergen—see page 13), and by no means all the cod nowadays is caught in Vestfjorden, the Lofot fishery has a special place in the folklore and literature of Norway.

A major change of the Norwegian fishing industry in this century has been in what happens to the fish after it is caught. Where once the bulk was dried (*stokkfisk*) or salted and dried (*klippfisk*) for export; now it is also canned or frozen, or transformed into cattle food, fertiliser, medicinal and other oils, fats for margarine, and other unlikely end products. In 1970, in terms of value, frozen fish fillets topped the export list of fish products (Kr463 million), followed by fish meal (Kr370 million), and by canned fish (Kr266 million). *Klippfisk* came fourth (Kr240 million) and *stokkfisk* sixth (Kr125 million).

Klippfisk (*klippe* = rock or cliff) are prepared by being split, heads and guts removed, and the rest salted and spread to dry on the smooth rocks of the strandflat. This leaves no sign for the summer visitor, which is perhaps as well, for the smell from January to May is said to reach far out to sea. *Stokkfisk* have head and guts removed and are then hung unsalted on those massive wooden frames that are a feature of the Lofot scene and of other northern ports (*plate 15*). Both methods retain a high nutritional content and allow the fish to be stored for years. It is a little surprising that such ancient ways of preserving fish persist to this degree.

The drying frames for *stokkfisk* vary in height, length and design. You can walk upright through the larger ones. They are guyed with wires to the surrounding rock, and weighted with rock suspended from other wires. In the season fish hang from them in enormous numbers, protected from the gulls by nets. The heads are turned into fish manure, the livers go for cod-liver oil, the roes are canned, and the gulls suffer indigestion for three months.

Cod and the Lofot fishery are now only a smallish part of Norway's oldest industry. Yet any statement about the relative importance, either in tonnage or kroner, of one breed of fish compared to another is apt to be confounded by the swift changes that can take place. For a time herring, mainly fished off the fjord coast of western Norway, was the major catch. In the 1950s it represented three-quarters of the annual total; by 1970 the proportion had dropped to a ninth. On the other hand the catch of capelin, a small fish found mainly off the northern coasts, seems to have risen sharply, from virtually none to half the catch of all fish in weight (not in value) in 1970. Capelin is processed for meal and oil. Mackerel, caught around the southern coasts in summer, is also declining, being roughly equal to the herring in value and weight in 1970. Among some fifty species fished, those caught in significant quantities include salmon, halibut, tuna, dogfish and the sprat or brisling. Dogfish is the 'rock salmon' of English fish-and-chip shops.

The sea also provides prawns, kelp (seaweed), seals and whales. Sealing is an old industry, now conducted mostly in distant waters off Newfoundland and Greenland. Whaling, once a major business in which the Norwegians led the world, has almost ceased.

It is not known whether the decrease of the cod, herring and mackerel shoals is due to overfishing or to natural causes, or a combination. The herring has a history of fickleness. For example, it favoured Bodø for the last thirty years or so of the nineteenth century, fortunes were made, and the town flourished. Then as suddenly the fish moved south, putting the town into a decline. The spawning herring needs a temperature of about 6°C; possibly the currents have changed, temporarily or permanently. There is no doubt, however, that present-day boats with modern equipment, aided by echo-sounding apparatus for tracking the shoals and by wireless and radio-telephone for passing information to the fishing fleets, have produced some vast catches, so that over-fishing must be suspected.

More than 90 per cent of Norway's fish are exported directly or in some processed form, and in 1970 made up about one-eighth of all exports. Fish are of far greater consequence to Norway than to the other Scandinavian lands. Thus an abatement of the source material is serious.

We left Kabelvåg at 3 pm for Lyngvær and the ferry to the next island, Vestvågøy. The clouds were down and rain showered. During the crossing the clouds sank lower and the rain fell torrentially. Although mountains closely surround this stretch of water, as we saw on our return, there was nothing to be seen now but rain-dippled waves and cloud, and nothing to do but wonder why the vast container lorry in front of the van had not sunk the ferry.

Smorten is a landing stage. We took route 815 along the south coast and stopped to make tea while the heavy rain wore itself out. About 5 pm the sky to the south-east did partially clear, and the cloud on the mountains began to shift and rise. From then on the sky changes were so swift and dramatic that we kept halting to watch. One could see cloud forming as invisible air currents from the sea hit the mountains, created little magical white wisps, and then, very quickly, thick streamers. I have a photograph taken at this moment looking back at Austvågøy, with a thin sunlight gleam on the precipices, and the cloud pouring horizontally from the peaks as though they were being consumed by massive internal fires.

This south-coast route down Vestvågøy is closely bordered by mountains. At several points the road is driven between enormous rocks, rocks as big as our van, piled up the slopes and down to and under the sea. Thus the evening search for a few flat yards continued for miles until, beyond Strandslett, we parked on a shallow loop of old road cut off by a recent straightening. There was no privacy, but traffic was thin and there was a compensating view of sea and rock peninsulas and cloud-swept mountain. The gulls cried in sudden squalls. When the tide came in, it lapped against the embankment of the new road, covering large areas of mud and rock, and floating all the limp seaweed into a beautiful three-dimensional forest.

The remainder of our time on Lofoten is quickly described. Next morning the cloud base was about 100ft and visibility about half a mile. It was raining hard as we drove down the peninsula to Stamsund, a modern fishing port whose site was blasted out of the mountainside at the beginning of the century. We needed a weather forecast. No one at the bank or the garage knew English, but a girl in the post office spoke it well. She asked us to return at 9.15, which we did, and learned that it would clear later. Good.

We decided to look at Ballstad near the southernmost tip of the island, reputed to be 'one of the loveliest spots in the whole of Lofoten'. It *was* lovely, even though we never saw the surrounding peaks. It lies at the end of a causeway joining former islands. There are several small separate anchorages on either side of tongues of rocky land. The south-east coasts of Austvågøy and Vestvågøy are a series of irregular-shaped peninsulas and promontories, with tidal creeks winding deep between them.

Ballstad's main harbour is surrounded not merely by the usual houses, dark-red sheds, jetties, quays and slipways, but by a thickset forest of fish-drying frames. These are sandwiched between houses and on the hillocks behind them, and they occupy every flattish rock within view, including several that are mere islets, whale backs in the middle of the harbour, where they provide fine perches for gulls. The spring stink must be horrific.

We sat in the van beside a stone quay drinking coffee while the rain poured down. During a twenty-minute break we climbed a hill and looked out over a few hundred yards of grey sea. The rain came on and we retreated to the van. A man emerged from the cabin of a fishing boat in jersey and trousers and pottered about the deck, oblivious of rain. We could not be. The rain exposed the limitations of life in a motorcaravan. When the object is to see sights and not to cover distance, rain prevents play; there is nothing to do but sit in the van or go where rain is not.

The speciality of Lofoten is the close combination of precipitous mountain and little fishing ports. The inability to see the one or explore the other was irritating. There seemed no point in moving on down the islands. So we decided to abandon them. The weather report from the girl in Stamsund's post office must have been optimistic.

But back on Austvågøy we came into sunshine. And after joining the queue at Svolvær for the 7 pm ferry to Skutvik on the mainland (there are four ferry trips in the twenty-four hours, one boat sailing eternally to and fro), it grew hot and the sky clear blue. Yesterday we had talked of spending three or four more days on the islands; now we were fleeing in perfect weather in half that time. Yet having made the decision, it was difficult to change. On long journeys the mind grows satiated with decision-making, occasionally rebels. We were tired, too easily lulled by the pleasure of lying stretched out on a bunk in the warm sun, from time to time gazing out at the activity in the square. Local boys mooch on bikes. Local teenagers slouch in

long-haired groups much as in England. The tourists in the ferry
queue perform a multitude of activities from eating to washing to
repacking to trying desperately to amuse small hot children. We did
walk up to the church, conspicuous on the hill close by. It was shut.

So those unvisited islands remain an accusation, a reproof, a
failure of will. For we should have turned round. The distances are
so short. I shall have to go back one day, reach down to Reine and to
Å, even if it thunders for the entire distance and I am sea-sick on
every ferry.

In compensation for this mild gloom, the voyage across Vestfjorden produced sights of rare beauty. It is a two-hour crossing over
open water, from north-west to south-east. For us the sea was calm,
the sky blue above a scattering of white cloud, and the sun was
preparing to think about setting.

As I have said, it is from the sea that the truly extraordinary nature
of Lofoten and the Vesterålen can be realised. As the ship moved out
of the harbour, the angle of the evening sun exaggerated the
shadows cast by those sweeping scrub-covered ridges and jagged
peaks, giving to them a sculptural quality, almost unreal in its
solidity. But by the time the ship had passed between the islands of
Skrova and Lille Molla, the peaks had receded, the chain had
lengthened, and the sun was set to set exactly behind Svolvær.
Finally, closing on Hamarøy, we looked back to a horizon of 100
miles of jagged peak and ridge, sometimes in several successive
layers, silhouetted black and grey by a red globe of sun resting
momentarily above Austvågøy and joined to us by a glittering red
path across the waves of our wake. Before us the mountains of
Hamarøy reached to 3,000ft, but these, less extravagantly formed,
were pink and mild by comparison with that distant black Lofot
wall.

Quietly we disembarked and in ten minutes found a disused sand
quarry for the night. The mind was full of images too brilliant to be
quickly overlaid.

8 Return to Trondheim

Route 81 from Skutvik to Ulsvåg, a post-war construction, is a pretty road down the length of the much-indented Hamarøy peninsula. On Hamarøy Knut Hamsun (1859-1952) spent his childhood. Next to Ibsen he is probably Norway's greatest modern writer and a Nobel Prize winner. The peninsula also owns wild raspberries; they were large and sweet.

There is an alternative route south from Skutvik that entails a mere 39 miles of driving but requires two long ferries. There is a ferry from Skutvik to Bogøy, followed by route 81 across the Steiga peninsula; another long ferry down Nordfolda and up the Sørfolda to Røsvik, and then the 20 miles to Fauske on route 826. The main road which we took is 105 miles (Skutvik to Fauske). The sea route, though it could well take longer and might cost more, would be restful and very beautiful.

We chose the main road, the Arctic Highway, because going north the scenery had been hidden by cloud and by rain, and I was still curious about 'the weird and sagalike beauty' (page 82). This time the weather was kinder, too kind, for a heat haze veiled the distant mountains, blotting some out entirely, mystifying others. But parts of the road *are* special. I recall particularly the sections on both sides of Kråkmo. There are a series of domes and buttresses of bare rock sweeping up from the valleys 2–3,000ft, each girdled by scree slopes like short skirts round a naked torso. The strata of the rock produce the most spectacular patterns. In Europe one does not often find land on this scale so denuded of vegetable cover. Though the physical world is made of shifting atoms and nothing now can be regarded as solid, this landscape must give some comfort to the uneasy traveller.

As we landed from the Bonnåsjøen-Sommarset ferry the rain began again; once more we passed through the six tunnels of the new section (page 104) and there was the sharp contrast of those dry surrealistic burrows banded with light and dark, followed by sudden soft rain-spattered evening views over the fjord far below. We had spent the whole morning in our private sand quarry near Skutvik. It was now quite late, time to find another sleeping spot.

Near a village called Evjo we turned east for a mile along a rough track, emerged from a wooded spur, and there lay before us a most beautiful lake. At this same point there was just room for the van to back off the track on to a grass siding. Over the bonnet the lake stretched in a long sickle curve to the right. In the foreground were green fields down to the shore; half a mile off there rose from the water a cirque of rock about 2,000ft high. There were three or four houses ahead of us, and a couple visible on the other bank. The water was clear and deep. Seagulls flew low above the surface and seemed to be catching insects. To one side a short wooded slope led to the falls by which the lake emptied into the head of the fjord. This was perhaps our most beautiful camp; not the best, for it was not sufficiently private, but the most beautiful.

Next day (10 August) we pushed on down the Highway, through Fauske and up the Saltdal valley as far as the turning east to Junkerdalen. We diverted ourselves up Junkerdalen for several hours, wanting somewhere to walk. The rain kindly eased for us, but back on the Highway it deluged, accompanied by thunder. It rained hard for the rest of the day's motoring. On the plateau by the Arctic Circle there were even remains of fresh snow near the road. Yet here the willow herb was still in flower. Driving long distances up and down Norway brings mental confusion as to the seasons, like air travel does for time. Flowers that are dying by the coast may be flourishing 2–300 miles to the south on a high plateau, and may be thick with seed in a neighbouring valley. Near Namsos next day we drove along roads misty with the white seed of willow herb floating across the fields. Indeed vegetation in Norway cannot safely be described by the region because it varies so rapidly according to soil, distance from the sea, height and temperature. These factors continually distort what one might expect from the degree of latitude. Norway is full of micro-climates.

Twelve miles short of Mo i Rana we turned east to climb the Grønfjelldal road and soon found a clearing 50 yards in, with the sound of Dunderfossen in the ear and a view west across the Dunderland valley to some long high ridges. The rain stopped, the clouds lifted, and there was even an attempt at sunshine. Moreover there were raspberries along the steep bank of the river, so that our supper of fresh fish from Fauske and fresh raspberries was for once wholly non-canned.

On a walk after supper up a logging track the abundance of wild raspberries was extraordinary, with fruit just as large and sweet as our English cultivated strains. The trees were conifers, darker and taller than any we had seen in recent days. Presumably they were Norway spruce. Much of the hillside we climbed had been felled and seemed to have been left to regenerate naturally. So far we had seen no forest plantations, though we had passed a couple of forest nurseries. The literature states that huge areas are being either replanted or planted for the first time, even north of the Arctic Circle.

In Mo i Rana next morning, with a day to spend in the area, we faced a choice. The efficient tourist office (in the square near the railway station), which forecast rain later, produced typed descriptions of the Grønli Caves and the Svartisen ice-cap. It was possible to tour the iron and steel works, A. S. Norsk Jernverk, at 10 am and 2 pm each day. There is a cable-car that carries bodies 1,350ft up Mount Mofjell. There is a museum. Or, more ambitious, we could drive along the Rana fjord, the 'Blue Road', 44 miles to Nesna, an ancient fishing village, and from there perhaps find a boat to some of the outer islands. There is Lovund, for example, with a colony of puffins.

We chose the ice-cap, or rather one of its glaciers. Svartisen means 'black ice'. It is Norway's second largest ice-cap, partly visible from the wide streets of Mo. The 22-mile approach route takes off from the E6 at Røssvoll, passes close to the airport, and then up Røssvoll-dalen and Svartisdalen to the east end of Lake Svartis. Here there is a car-park and café, and a motorboat on the hour every hour to the west end of the lake. The road is not a good one, but it is beautiful; indeed the river, swollen with the recent rain and grey-green with melt-water from the ice-cap, was surging over the grass and through the tree trunks along the banks and was quite alarmingly impressive.

The motorboat takes a noisy twenty minutes to cross the lake. The lower flanks of the valley are wooded, absorbing dozens of waterfalls that stream down the bare higher slopes. From the far landing stage it is a forty-minute climb up and along a rocky path, and the snout of the glacier is hidden until near the end.

The Svartisen has been retreating. At the turn of the century the Østerdalsisen, the glacier which we now inspected, ended in the lake, and the Engabreen to the west reached almost to the sea. Yet in the eighteenth century both were growing. With predictions that our climate is turning to a colder phase, perhaps the great retreat will halt and the ice may advance again down these scoured valleys.

The melt-water from the Østerdalsisen is conducted in a most civilised way down a tunnel; there is no torrent roaring from the snout. Instead there are dozens of small, still lakes or pools in the hollows of the ice-scraped rock. The snout is remarkable for a series of caverns in the ice which it is possible to explore. The exterior ice is dirty, mixed with black grit, but inside the ice is clean and marvellous shades of blue. It is blue because, as the buried snow of the glacier gets more densely packed and re-crystallises into ice, it loses air bubbles and its whiteness. Presumably these ice caverns are a by-product of the rapid melting. Certainly one needs protec-tion against the massive dripping that makes their exploration a

Page 107   (above) 20 *farmland in winter, not far from Oslo, to remind the
summer visitor that thick snow covers the whole country every year for varying
periods* (page 57); (below) 21 *Telemark scenery in summer, taken from route 45
near the border with Aust-Agder* (page 162)

Page 108   Oslo: (above) 22 the small-ships harbour with Rådhuset, the city hall,
on the right and the white ski-jump at Holmenkollen (page 148) just visible on the
hillside towards the left; (below) 23 modern flats in a western suburb (page 152);
each has a small patio on the roof of the one below, with a view over the city and
the fjord

damp affair. It is an odd feeling to stand upon rock that until quite recently has been submerged beneath ice for thousands and thousands of years.

From the snout of the glacier there is nothing to be seen of the ice-cap. It would be better to allow several hours for climbing the bordering rock, which looks negotiable, and hope to achieve a viewpoint. Svartisen is divided by an ice-free valley, and there is a path through the valley marked on the map. That path might make a fine expedition for walkers. They could step over the Arctic Circle, which cuts the southern edge of the ice-cap.

To reach the Grønli caves one starts on the same route from Mo as for the Svartisen, but where the glacier road turns to cross the Rovatnet on a bridge, the Grønligrotten road goes straight on. We did not visit the caves. They are well spoken of, with a variety of caverns, passages and peculiar rock formations, and with that item essential to every self-respecting set of caves, an underground river. They are limestone caves, enlarged by glacial action, and not the only ones in the area.

Mo i Rana is a modern industrial town created by an act of State out of a fishing village and local market centre. It lies at the head of the Rana fjord. The great Norsk Jernverk iron and steel plant was opened here in 1955, as part of the government's postwar plan for developing North Norway. The Dunderland valley, where we had spent the previous night, is loaded with iron, but the iron-content of the ore is low and for years there were technical difficulties with the processing. These have been overcome and Norsk Jernverk now uses this local ore as well as ore from Norway's largest iron mines near the Russian border at Kirkenes (rebuilt with Marshall Aid funds after their destruction in the war).

At Mo also is the Norsk Koksverk, which sounds more impressive than 'Norwegian Cokeworks'. It uses coal from Spitzbergen. A new power station, built into a mountain, supplies electricity to the area. As a result the town has increased in size from about 1,500 people in 1930 to over 10,000, and shows many obvious signs of prosperity—a lot of new stores under construction, for example.

G

I think we made a mistake in choosing the glacier and not the iron and steel works. Anyone who has seen a glacier elsewhere will not see anything especially new up at Svartisen, unless he be a specialist. On the other hand to understand modern Norway the visitor should look over one or other of the great industrial plants, and we missed our chance at Mo.

From Mo, route 77 goes east 25 miles to the Swedish border. This route was completed during the war (it had been a well-used track), and is the most northerly road direct into Sweden. We decided to explore it, re-entering Norway on route 76, thus seeing a corner of Sweden's vast northern territories, and avoiding a section of the E6 already covered.

When we left Mo at 4.15 pm it was raining hard and the road turned out to have an execrable surface, continuous linked pot-holes which were impossible to avoid. It was being 'improved' in such a truly whole-hearted fashion that it was almost unnegotiable. According to John Douglas (*The Arctic Highway*, 80), this always was a bad road, but is being regraded and widened so that the Swedes may export timber through Mo. It climbs to over 2,000ft at the frontier.

We drove for 20 miles or so into Sweden, mostly beside Lake Øveruman. Short stretches of tar alternated with long stretches of earthy holes and bumps. The rain stopped, allowing views of distant snow peaks. For the car-camper there is a further disagreeable by-product of road improvement: all the small informal tracks that over the years for one purpose or another are driven into the surrounding countryside get interrupted, cut off. The car-camper comes to rely on these for a private night's sleep. For our night we had to settle for a piece of abandoned road parallel with the new alignment and only 50 yards off.

Next day (12 August) the driving was much improved. From the end of Lake Øveruman to the junction with route 76 there was good new tar, freeing the driver to look at the scenery.

This distant corner of Swedish Lapland is suddenly and quite obviously different from Norway, from that long narrow strip of

Norway north of Trondheim. This eastern side of the mountain divide is spacious, with wide skies, rolling forested hills, lakes that are not imprisoned by bare mountains, and rivers that are not a continuous cascade.

It is a gap in my education that I am unable to distinguish a piece of Baltic Shield from a section of Caledonian Fold. I have to accept untested the fact that 90 per cent of Finland, 75 per cent of Sweden and the southern parts of Norway are formed of Baltic Shield, ancient rock of the Archaean age, overlaid now with the clays, sands and gravels left by the Quaternary ice-sheet. This rock has been worn down over the millennia to a vast sloping plateau or plain reaching from the Norwegian mountains to the coast at the Gulf of Bothnia.

Much of Norway, on the other hand, consists of mountains folded during the Caledonian period, formed of sediments that had accumulated previously along the western and northern flanks of the Baltic Shield. Movements in the earth's crust squeezed and crushed and pushed these sediments against the Shield until they rose high above it and sometimes over it, forming a scarp or ridge that lies close to the political boundary between Norway and Sweden, at least in the north.

This is to simplify grossly. There have been complications. For one, over the millennia the earth seems to have risen and sunk like a cork in a tidal basin, the seas have flowed in and out, and fresh cycles of erosion have again and again begun their task of democratic levelling. There are parts of Sweden that are now 900ft above the sea that were submerged as recently as 7,500 BC. And the sites of most known early ports are now inland, literally stranded by the rising of the earth.

But this brief geological foray does perhaps begin to account for the contrast between the abrupt mountains and fjords of north and western Norway, and the forest-covered expanses of the plains of Sweden.

It is tempting to go farther, to use this basic geographic fact to explain the differences between the Swedish and Norwegian peoples. It is odd, when you stare at a map, that the Scandinavian peninsula should be divided politically in the way it is, and that, by and large, the divisions have lasted for at least 2,000 years. Geography, one feels, must hold much of the answer. For it is only yesterday that our technical age has allowed peoples to begin to shape their lives in apparent disregard of rock and soils and climate. However these are dangerous waters for a novice seaman and perhaps it is best to stand away.

The Swedes dry their hay differently, at least they do along their route 361. Instead of long lines of wire stretched between posts (*plate 11*), they build little individual racks of wood, like a clothes horse, about 5ft high and 6–10ft long. A field of these, each stuffed with hay, looks a little as though it is populated by a herd of strange shaggy beasts. But this is not a book about Sweden and I must proceed swiftly to the road junction at Västansjö, where we turned west to regain Norway after a night and 58 miles of delightful driving in a foreign land.

The border provided the most reticent frontier post of my experience—a short stone pillar beside the road. Again it was almost on the watershed. On the Norwegian side the road immediately narrowed, the landscape soon rose abruptly, and it began to rain. It rained off and on in short bursts until late afternoon, which spoilt picnics but gave us magnificent sunlit clouds.

Route 76 turned out to be a good scenic drive, and the surface good waterbound gravel. No one anywhere was trying to improve it. At one point it passes close to an arm of Lake Røsvatn, Norway's second largest lake. Southwards the enormous bump of Mount Hatten (3,700ft) rises in isolation. At or near the village of Hattfjelldal, where there is an airport, several roads take off into the valleys and hills. They include a route into Sweden. Here would be yet another area worth exploring slowly over several days.

We reached Vegset and the E6 at midday, having dropped from 1,970ft to 230ft since that frontier stone. We spent the next few hours bounding south along the E6, stopping only to look at Trongfossen, a spectacular gorge and waterfall in the Namsen river just south of Flatådal. From the road a number of rough peaty paths lead through heather, bushes and trees to the edge of the gorge. There is nothing to prevent you from falling over, no railings, no cautionary notice; and there is no entrance charge. A man is free to go where he wills and to fall 400ft if he is tired of life. I count this one of Norway's blessings. The edge of the gorge was rich with bilberry bushes, and the berries too were free.

Short of Grong we turned west on to route 760. The intention was to reach Trondheim by way of Namsos and the peninsula that forms the north bank of Trondheimsfjorden. There is a ferry from Vanvikan to Trondheim.

It was late, so 3 miles along route 760 we turned up the side road to Føynum, and after a mile branched aside to nose along a farm track beside a small river. On occasions like this it is wise to do a foot reconnaissance ahead of the van to make sure that there is somewhere to park and turn. We found a clearing in the woods that allowed us off the track, and so settled down.

This was a very private and satisfactory site in a beautiful and un-Norwegian corner of the country. The rain had stopped, and after supper we explored. The land was an eruption of small broken hills, steep but round-topped, some forested, some cleared and covered with thick tall golden-headed grass. The valley was clay, yet the slow-moving stream (and we never saw another stream moving slowly in Norway) was peat-brown overhung with trees and bushes. We climbed a hill. On a bare spur of an opposite ridge a group of white and red farm buildings stood out clear and clean in contrast to the dark forest, and beyond that in the distance was the long rock ridge that borders the far bank of the Namsen river.

In the middle of a flat field by the river where the grass had just been harvested, a field surrounded by hills, was a mound, circular, perhaps 60ft high, steep, grass-covered, obviously artificial. For those who know Silbury Hill in Wiltshire, it was a miniature version of that. Next morning a young man on a tractor with limited

English said: 'They not know what it is, but it is for burial.' So at last, and by accident, we saw a burial mound, one of our own finding and thus three times as beneficial. As to the date, Anders Hagen (*Norway*, 150) writes: 'Of the grand total of some 200,000 prehistoric sites and monuments [in Norway] the majority are grave mounds, and of these a large proportion date from the Late Iron Age, especially from its last phase, the Viking Age. Late Iron Age mounds were usually built of earth and rubble. They are circular in plan, domed . . .' Our mound meets this description, except that it is higher than the '13–20 feet' that Hagen says is typical.

Next morning, starting late, we drove into Namsos. But first route 17 must be mentioned. By combining route 805 (the Blue Road) with route 17 and the roads we traversed later on this day, it is possible to drive from Mo i Rana to Trondheim without touching the E6, the Arctic Highway. I had intended to do this coming south, but the persistent rain, which tends to be worse near the coast, put us off, and we did the Swedish diversion eastwards instead. There are seven ferries on this sea route (six north of Namsos, one to the south), which therefore takes time, but it passes through marvellous coastal scenery, close to several famous Stone Age, viking and medieval sites, and has other tempting diversions.

Until this century it was the coast that mattered; inland communication was poor and discontinuous. The island of Tjøtta, for example, was an important place in viking times, and at one period later had 200–300 farms and a famous manor house. At Alstahaug to the north is one of Norway's finest small early medieval churches, noted as the home of the seventeenth-century poet-priest Petter Dass. In good weather this route should be given high priority in planning.

On either side of Namsos route 17 passes through rich farming country—it appears rich by comparison with the north. We had a sunny day for a change, and the fields of oats and barley were golden ripe. It was rolling hill country, intricate with spurs, ridges and odd hillocks. The heights were wooded, the lower slopes cultivated. And on many a spur, standing out because of the red and ochre and white paint, are the grouped farm buildings. In England farm buildings tend to merge with the land, being made of grey stone or mellowed brick. In Norway they are made of wood, and nearly always painted in colours that contrast with the land.

The farms here had their living quarters painted white. They were long buildings with eight or even ten pairs of windows in two storeys. There was usually a window in the gable end of the roof, and sometimes cellar windows are visible. In the Namsen valley some of these houses were obviously old and of a most gracious design. Close to the white living house are one or more barns, equally large, usually painted a dark red, occasionally ochre or left as natural wood. The older farms form a close square, with a gap at one corner. Newer farms are more open, making a rectangle, or with a barn in parallel.

It was surprising how close the farms were to one another. It did not seem possible that each could make a living from so little land so far north. *Facts about Norway* says that of the 146,000 farms with more than one acre, only 24,000 have more than 25 acres, and only forty have more than 250 acres; 49,000 farms, about a third, completely support their owners. Other owners have other occupations. The demand for labour is so seasonal that 'almost 95 per cent of the work is done by the farmer himself and his family'. Most farms are owner-occupied; tenant farmers are uncommon.

Considering how important milk is to the economy (half of it is made into cheese, butter, etc), it was surprising how seldom we had seen cows. On the higher pastures sheep were common. And on almost every farm of any size there are to be seen somewhere pieces of machinery which we named 'triffids' (after the walking plants of John Wyndham's *The Day of the Triffids*), for they stand very upright, have a swivel head with a large mouth, and an air of intelligent questing as though waiting to eat people (*plate 12*). These are forage harvesters. They are pulled by tractors through a field of grass which they cut, chop, lacerate and spit out into a trailer in one continuous movement. The result is put into silos. In 1959 there were none of these beasts; in 1971 there were 18,000. Their numbers reflect the importance of forage to the farming economy, and the fact, obvious as you drive along, that grass is grown as a crop for hay and forage (47 per cent of the agricultural acreage) far more than for pasture (18 per cent). Grains too are mostly grown for animals. Barley and oats predominate. This is a consequence of the long winters when the earth is frozen and animals are stall-fed on hay and other preserved foods.

Like Britain, Norway is not self-sufficient in food. There just is not enough good soil to feed 4 million mouths.

Namsos is a timber town. In the centre are streets of shops and offices, and a modern church, and houses. But at either end are acres of stacked timber, and along the waterfront the wharves are made of timber, and the sheds on the wharves are full of timber, and timber floats in parts of the harbour. The neat stacks of sawn timber are up to 10–12ft high, each stack raised off the ground and capped with a roof of corrugated iron. It is as if an industrious child had been at play with giant matchsticks.

The centre of the town was wrecked by bombs in April 1940. The houses were made of wood and burned well, as did the wharves and the rolling stock on the railway. Thus everything has a new look. Denied the timber-crowded flats, the town has been expanding up the lower slopes of the confining hills.

We spent the afternoon getting ourselves to Vanvikan, opposite Trondheim, via route 17 and then route 720. The map is out of date: there was asphalt on all but a mile or so of route 720. The whole drive through this unfrequented peninsula is pretty, but the section along Beitstadfjorden is especially so.

At Vanvikan for the first time there was a long queue for the ferry, despite a sailing every twenty minutes. It was a Sunday evening, and obviously half of Trondheim had been weekending on our side of the fjord. So we spent the night a few miles along the

coast and next morning caught an early ferry. It is proper to enter a
port by sea and one should always contrive to do so. Trondheim,
though half veiled by a morning mist, takes on a third dimension
when seen from the water.

9 Røros and the Eastern Border

We left Trondheim for Røros in the early afternoon. The E6 out of Trondheim is one of the more crowded roads, a jam of slow-moving traffic on this occasion. To turn off it on to route 30 at Støren was a relief. From the junction it is 63 miles to Røros, climbing gently up Gauldalen along with the railway. This railway was the first of the two lines to Oslo to be completed (1880) and the impulse for its construction was partly the copper at Røros.

Copper is not the only mineral in the region. The guidebooks say that the pyrites mines at Killingdal, whose surface at 2,970ft is visible high on an eastern mountain from the road near Unsholtet, reaches down to 790ft below sea-level. One cannot help being impressed by a fact of this kind, though it is hard to say why. Pyrites (a composite ore) is one of the two most profitable ores mined in Norway (iron is the other), and the largest of the pyrites mines is not far away at Løkken in Orkladalen, the most western of the valleys that converge on Trondheim. Copper, lead and zinc are extracted from pyrites. But it is sulphur that is most important; this is processed into sulphuric acid.

We spent the night in some old stone workings at about 2,000ft, nearly the highest point on the road. The trees were short again and birchy, the soil was peaty, and there was heather in flower. For the first time for many days the ground was really dry. We saw a number of cows. Some had their horns capped with red balls, and some had wildly irregular horns—one curving up and one down,

for example, like some drunken reveller whose fancy-dress has run
into trouble.

Eastern Norway is far drier than the north, west and south. It is
really one great upland plateau dissected by several long north-
south valleys that drain into the Oslo fjord. These valleys are
important in Norwegian culture and history. Røros is on the
plateau. It is close to Lake Aursund, the source of Norway's longest
river (380 miles), the Glomma, sometimes spelt Glåma. From Røros
one can follow the Glomma by road for most of its course to its
mouth at Fredrikstad, south of Oslo.

Røros lies in a shallow basin. Although the hills around it are
partly wooded, the general impression is of barrenness. It is not
surprising to learn that the climate is very cold in winter, colder
than almost any other inhabited part of Norway except for the
inland areas of Finnmark in the extreme north, and that it is well
inside those upland and northern areas where the snow lies for more
than 180 days in the year. Along the south-west coast the snow
cover lasts less than thirty days.

It was in 1644 that copper was discovered and the town was
founded. Since then it has been continuously mined, though now on
a small scale with under a hundred men. Røros was the only town
we visited whose population has not increased in recent years; it has
remained at about 3,000. Røros was also that rare phenomenon in
Norway, a tourist town—organised for tourists and living mainly on
tourists. The place is stuffed with hotels and camp sites. Tourists are
brought in by the coachload to look at the old mining street—
preserved like a mummy and about as lively—at the copper-mine
museum, and at the mines themselves, which are outside the town.

On the Quintus mine the leaflet in English says: 'The whole
setting breathes that uncanny air of drama that surrounded the lives
of the copper mines. Here a remarkable chapter in the history of
Norway has literally been hewn out of rock.' That sort of souped-up
patter is common enough over much of tourist Europe, and if you
are keen on copper mines, do not let it put you off. But it put us off.
We did not go down the mine and I found the Copper Mine

Collection rather dull. The houses in the old mining street were all shut, opening only to conducted tours.

The best things in Røros for me were Domus (the Department store), the church, and the crusty bread we bought in Bergmanns-gata. We came late to the Domus shops. We had discovered them only the day before on the return through Trondheim. The English comparison would be a cross between Marks & Spencer and Woolworths, with a café and excellent washrooms thrown in. Domus sell just about everything that a family commonly requires and at reasonable prices. They are self-service, so the visitor needs no battle with language to search for his wants. Trondheim has a vast Domus not far from the Ringve Museum. Røros has a modest one, but the washroom had scalding water, soap and paper towels, and the lavatory had a little heater (evidence of the winter climate). These small luxuries mean so much to the motorcaravanner that he will cover miles to enjoy them. There is not a Domus in every town. But almost every town and many smaller centres have a Cooperative Society store (Samvirkelag), the shop-front plastered with the easily recognised 'S'. These seemed to us to be like a poor cousin of the Domus shops, but equally useful for everyday needs.

The church at Røros is very fine. It figures prominently in most photographs of the town (*plate 16*). It is of stone and brick, painted black and white outside except for the roof of wooden shingles and a green dome with spire that caps the tower. Inside it is a shock of blue. There are double galleries on either side, like a theatre. An elaborate pulpit in white and gold projects over the altar, and above the pulpit is the baroque organ from the seventeenth century. The church was dedicated in 1784. Some of the pews are curtained, a reminder of the copper 'establishment', part of the class hierarchy that Norway has been more successful in removing than Britain. The portraits are interesting. And it is worth wandering up the hill through the surprisingly unkempt graveyard to the modern burial chapel at the top. This has an accompanying bell-tower built of enormous round boulders.

The centre of the town has some nice streets with seventeenth-century painted wooden houses. Here is one town that has not been burnt down too recently. The Røros museum, which is a little way out, has cottage furniture, local costume, and a stuffed reindeer pulling a sledge shaped like a boat.* In the town there are preserved some fine slag heaps.

For reasons which escape me the town has a mystique for many Norwegians that its physical presence hardly seems to support. For them industrialisation came late and in small packets, and perhaps Røros provides one of the very few examples in their lovely land of eighteenth- and nineteenth-century industrial hell. Or perhaps it exudes romantic memories of the early copper-rush fever that drew fortune-seekers from all over Europe. Or perhaps, for Norwegians, the novels of Johan Falkberget are as the novels of Charles Dickens to the English-speaking world, or those of Emile Zola to the French. Falkberget (1879–1967) was born in Røros, the son of a miner, and wrote a series of historical novels set in the area that are highly regarded.

From Røros route 31 leads east to the Swedish province of Härjedalen. We followed the Glomma river downstream for 8 miles, then turned south on to route 26, which runs more or less parallel with the frontier. The surface is gravel to Brenna, then tar for some miles, then gravel again.

I do not know how typical of the frontier area to the south this section may be, for we left it at the Isterfoss waterfall to turn west on route 217. It is curious country, with the road almost level at around 2,000ft for 55 miles. Tufsingdalen is especially notable. It was muted, sad (there was a grey overcast sky), scattered with scrubby silver birch or small pine. Moss and lichen were everywhere, grey, brown, light green and dull yellow. There was a lot of heather in flower. In some areas acres of great grey rocks were scattered

* The majority of reindeer in Scandinavia and Siberia are owned and marked; although semi-wild, they are controlled. Both sexes have antlers. Reindeer are ridden and used as pack animals, as well as sledge-drawers.

haphazardly. Often boulders line the road and surround the fields from which they have been cleared. This does not look a happy farming area; and there were not many fields visible from the road.

Where woodland had been felled, the gentle hillsides were dotted with tree stumps and strewn with dead twisted branches. The soil is either sandy, or peat and bog. When we stopped to photograph the lichen, which is very beautiful, we were attacked by mosquitoes in larger cohorts than anywhere during the journey.

Next morning, in the Rena valley (route 3), we stopped to look at Ytre Rendal church at Otnes, built in 1752, perhaps typical of these small eighteenth-century country churches, though no two are alike. The basic structure is of logs, visible inside, but on the outside sheathed with vertical planking painted terracotta. The whole structure rests on a dry-stone foundation to lift the wood clear of the earth. There is a porch, and bits added on elsewhere. And there is a slender steeple covered with black shingles, with an attractive bulbous section where it emerges from a short tower.

The church was open because workmen were fitting a new organ; pieces of the old one lay about outside and in the porch. The interior was brightly painted in blue, with red and green and grey trimmings. The font and pulpit had painted canopies. The altar had a crucifixion scene carved in wood. The box pews, which are common everywhere, were painted grey-blue with terracotta edgings. There was a generous gallery, stretching over a third of the inside, and it was up there that the workmen were installing the new organ.

The Rena valley here is narrow and deep, clothed with conifers on both sides from bottom to top. Not far to the south it swings west to join Østerdalen and the Glomma river. At Øvre Rendal we left the Rena to cross into Østerdalen. This little country road of 11 miles is well worth doing. It was constructed in 1879—according to the stone plaques at either end, each with an elaborate royal monogram carved on it. The road climbs 1,000ft or so over the intervening plateau, and if you have been stuck in the valleys for some while you need a bit of open air.

Up on the plateau we passed a group of beehives, painted white. We had seen others earlier on high ground among the heather. There is a great deal of heather in Norway, and in 1969 there were, if everybody sent in their returns correctly, 51,912 beehives.

Østerdalen is the most easterly of Norway's great valleys. It is a valley of forests, spruce and pine, with a fringe of birch at the upper tree line. There are only a few small farms, for the tree is king. We moved down Østerdalen for a mere 8 miles, for we meant to traverse yet farther west to the grandest of all the valleys, Gudbrandsdalen. Thus at Atna we turned on to route 27 past wood and farm in the Atna river valley until the road began to climb and climb, leaving the river far below. At Sollia (2,240ft) there were wide views south over forested ridges to mountains of 4,000ft. Up here for the first time we met timber lorries, two large ones in quick succession. The wise traveller gives them immediate precedence. On this day too we saw a number of those lovely dun horses that enrich the landscape. Alas their number is decreasing fast as the tractors take over.

Route 27 leads on, after Enden, to Folldal, Hjerkinn and the Dovrefjell; earlier we had travelled the latter half after our night in Grimsdalen (page 55). This time we turned south at Enden on to route 220. From 2,300ft the road climbs another 1,000ft. Near the highest point, in the middle of moorlands, we stopped and walked.

There were marked paths across the moors in several directions. It is easy to be independent, to pioneer a line of one's own; but the chances are high that you will get blocked by a bog. For this is curious country: boggy moorlands from which rise stone-sheathed mountains, the Rondane mountains.

We were drawn on, and instead of a quick trot of half an hour, climbed a mountain. This began with a stiff ascent over stone and shale and bare earth. The final 500ft were up a close-knit mass of rock and boulder that covered the summit dome. The rock was coloured a vivid green from lichen; it was a green mountain, even from a mile away. On the top were innumerable cairns. There was a marvellous view and a cold wind, with spatters of rain.

At this level one can generally see for a long way and until interrupted by higher mountains, which did not happen here for 30 miles in some directions. The whole panorama appears to be plateau and peak. The narrow valleys in which man must spend most of his life are scarcely visible, mere shadows across the bleak moors. Even the great Gudbrandsdal a few miles to the south-west was no more than a dark line. From here Norway is a wilderness. The books say so, the maps show it, but to understand it you must climb a peak from time to time, and watch civilisation vanish.

Back in the van we had just got going, tired but rewarded, when we were hit by a storm: rain, thunder, and then thick hail that brought us to a halt. In the Alps I had once seen caravans pock-marked from hail, and they had been stationary. The noise was forbidding, a continuous charge of buckshot on a tin roof.

In good weather the descent into Gudbrandsdalen and to Ringebu must be spectacular. We saw little but the surface of the road. We went to look at Ringebu stave church—off the E6 up a steep track south of the village and open from 10 am to 6 pm. My postcard says: 'first mentioned in 1270 but is older'. Originally it was of the cruciform basilica plan. It was rebuilt in 1620, when it acquired its pointed spire, chancel and transepts. Only the nave is original. There are massive columns of wood, intricately painted, rising to a considerable height; and a triforium of horse-shoe arcading, almost Moorish; and above these the usual complex structure of struts and beams. It was a wet, dark evening, so we saw the church looking dimly mysterious, closer than usual to its original state, when there would have been few or no windows.

Page 125 (above)
24 *Edvard Munch: a self-portrait of 1905 (page 140)*;
(below) 25 *one of the several ladies who adorn the public garden outside Rådhuset in Oslo (page 146)*

(above) 26 *industry above the Arctic Circle: the Norsk Hydro plant at Glomfford (page 159). A few years ago there was nothing there; (below) 27 an offshore oil-storage tank leaving Stavanger for the North Sea in 1973; eventually it will rest on the sea bed. Oil tankers form a large part of Norway's merchant fleet, which is a prime earner of foreign currency. Now the production of oil itself may become a major factor in the economy*

10 Lillehammer
South to Oslo

We woke to a high wind and to rain, and reluctantly abandoned the 'Peer Gynt' road. This is a toll road through the mountains to the west of the Gudbrandsdal, much of it above the tree line. It leaves the E6 at Vinstra, a few miles north of Ringebu, and rejoins either at Tretten or Fåberg. The E6 in the valley is a fast road, and the scenery fine, but I would always choose a mountain route so long as time and clouds permit.

The commercialisation of Peer Gynt proceeds apace. No doubt it was inevitable that Ibsen's creation—a character firmly rooted in the Norwegian countryside, despite his voyaging, and a character partly based on local legends of a real person who had lived in the Gudbrandsdal about a hundred years earlier—should be thus exploited. There are Peer Gynt Hotels, Peer Gynt cottages, several Peer Gynt monuments, and so on.

Gudbrandsdalen north of Ringebu penetrates between two great mountain plateaux, Rondane and Jotunheimen, and then rises to its source in a third, the Dovrefjell. This vast complex of moorland, mountain peak and deep valley is the physical heart of Norway, and it is the Peer Gynt country.

For us it was raining hard and clouds were capping every ridge. We drove straight down Gudbrandsdalen to Lillehammer. Along much of this historic valley the farms climb right up the hillside, not continuously, for there are patches and strips of forest in between, but over a far greater area than in Østerdalen to the east. The valley floor, with the river Lågen a soapy green colour, is wider than most, rich with meadows lying on glacial terraces and deltas. Indeed Gudbrandsdalen is probably the most fertile of the great valleys; it was the line of very early inland penetration and settlement from the coast. It is said that there are farming families who can trace their occupation of farms here back to the ninth century. The valley carries the traditional route to Trondheim and the north, and has always been used by travellers and by armies.

Lillehammer is at the mouth of Gudbrandsdalen and on the shores of Lake Mjøsa, Norway's largest lake (142 square miles). The lake is never wide; it stretches south-east almost for ever and somewhere is nearly 1,500ft deep. In the old days travellers covered this part of the route by boat. When Mattieu Williams did the trip, it was in a steamer owned by a Scotsman, and the second-class fare was 17p. Nowadays one goes by rail or road, which is a deterioration. But there is an old paddle-steamer operating for tourists between Minnesund and Lillehammer that has been crossing the lake since 1856, and so could be the boat used by Mr Williams (his preface is dated 1859).

Lillehammer is now a major tourist town, summer and winter, with a population of about 20,000. It was still pouring rain when we reached it, weather for art-gallery visiting. The gallery is at one end of a modern building, most of which is a cinema, a *kino*. It is a good art gallery, spacious, uncluttered and not too large. For anyone wanting a quick conspectus of the range of Norwegian art from the mid-nineteenth century to the present day, this gallery would serve well. There is a small selection of works by contemporary artists for sale. We sampled the *kino* that evening, and sat through *Ben Hur* with an audience wholly composed of blonde boys and blonde girls impossible to tell apart until they spoke. It was a surrealistic experience.

That afternoon and the next morning we spent in the Sandvig Collections at Maihaugen. Started by Anders Sandvig, a dentist, in 1887, the open-air part alone contains about 100 buildings with 30,000 items inside them, and the large new exhibition hall houses many thousands of additional objects. What the museum attempts to do, through examples taken mostly from Gudbrandsdalen, is 'to show life, as it was lived, in all its variety: how the country people of Norway lived, built and worked, and how they enjoyed their leisure hours, through the ages'. It is a museum of historical culture. If you reach Lillehammer, as we did, after several weeks of wandering, weeks at least partly spent in trying to understand what the eye beheld, here at Maihaugen things begin to fall into place, to connect, to make sense. The collections perform comprehensively what the many little open-air museums elsewhere, such as those we visited at Voss and Vågåmo, achieve in part.

The setting is a hillside of birch and conifers, several lakes and small streams. Into this have been fitted buildings of all types and from many centuries: valley and mountain farms large and small, fishermen's huts, a *stavkirke* and a chapel, a schoolhouse, a parsonage, a local arsenal, and so on. These are not, except for the stave church, modern reconstructions. They are actual buildings, whose location and history are known, that have been taken down and rebuilt. The interiors are furnished in appropriate styles. The result, if one takes a little time, is a voyage into the past that is absorbing.

There is nothing grandiose here, hardly a hint of Versailles, Vienna or Rome. Here are shown the achievements of a country people, living always close to mountain and forest, self-reliant. Wood and cloth, simple colour schemes in paint and dye, are the basis of their craft. With these they made an astonishing variety of objects, not sophisticated, a little rough, but strong and satisfying. The industrial revolution came late to the inland valleys of Norway, and Anders Sandvig was able to find examples in abundance that in other countries had vanished before their value was realised.

Amongst much else, at Maihaugen it is possible to study the architectural development of the log house. *Stav* work, as already explained, used vertical logs, held rigid top and bottom by tie beams; it was employed mostly for churches. *Laft* work laid logs horizontally one upon another, and dovetailed together at the corners; it was used for domestic buildings. Until the arrival of the water-driven saw in the sixteenth century, it was easier to use whole logs; for hundreds of years afterwards it was cheaper to do so because of the scarcity of mills and the expense of nails.

Norway was never, like England, a land of villages. There were scarcely any merchants, few artisans, no 'middle class'. It was a land of individual farms, and the developing skills in the use of wood for buildings can be studied through the developing complexity of the log houses on the farms. It is thought by some that the American log cabin derives from early Scandinavian emigrants.

Farms were self-supporting and consisted of anything from four or five to thirty buildings; a dozen or so were common. From the simplest one-room hut to houses with two storeys, several rooms on each, and galleries; from the open central hearth with a smoke-hole in the roof to the iron stove and a chimney flue; from a beaten earth floor to close-fitting, draught-proof planking; from no windows to large glass panes; from bench to chair; from axe to saw and plane—all such developments can be seen at Maihaugen. They reflect not merely the increasing wealth and skill of a particular family, but of a whole society, a nation.

This is the story, too, of the changing conditions of life for most people in Europe. Though materials, techniques and designs differed, and time-spans varied, the same broad stages must have been common. And in North America the phrase 'from log cabin to White House' can be seen as more than a reference to one man in his own lifetime.

Eventually there was skill and time and wealth to spare for luxuries: for intricate wood-carving, for joinery, for wall tapestries (which keep out draughts as well as decorate), for painted designs on cupboards, for 'rose painting' on walls and doors, for clocks, and even for imported objects. In Gudbrandsdalen wood-carving was especially rich. It is important to see household furniture and utensils in context, in the rooms as they were used and not as objects packed close in a museum; this you can do at Maihaugen.

Mention ought to be made of one type of building, typical over so much of Norway that it could almost be the country's symbol. This is the *stabbur* or loft or storehouse. Where communities have no central storage system (shops, warehouses), each unit must itself store for the winter and for lean years. *Stabbur* were built with two storeys long before living houses; homes were restricted to one storey until the arrival of chimneys (which began to come in during the sixteenth century, but were not in general use until the seventeenth). The second storey of the *stabbur* usually overhangs the first, with an encircling balcony. A great deal of skilled carving might be lavished on the exterior. In some districts, especially Telemark, the *stabbur* are architectural showpieces, carefully preserved.

Maihaugen has an upper level with three delightful lakes and examples set around them of mountain farms and other buildings of the hills. The guided visitor on a quick schedule may miss these, which would be a pity. (A guided tour is necessary at some point, for most of the fully furnished houses of the lower farms are locked until a guided party reaches them.)

The use of mountain pasturage was essential to the economy of the valley farms, for in the valleys the land was used to grow grain for people and hay for the working horses. The cows and goats, stall-fed on starvation rations all winter, staggered to the high pastures in the late spring and were only expected to give milk during the summer. Mountain lakes provided fish, mountain forest and moorland held game for trapping; both these sources of food were more important formerly than now.

A mountain or summer farm is called a *seter*. The high valleys and plateaux are dotted with *seter*. The word is always cropping up in the literature. A *seter* can be anything from a one-room hut to a building with several rooms and accompanying stables, byres, haylofts, etc. My friend Mattieu Williams spent a night in a rough *seter* whose sole occupant was 'a ruddy, muscular, rural beauty', the dairymaid. This one slept by day, and while M.W. used her bed, spent the evening milking and the night making cheese and butter. The milking was done in a nearby building, but the cheese-making was done in the same 15ft by 12ft room. At 5 am when he left 'she was at work again, making more cheese from the morning's milking'.

Since the cows gave no milk through the long winter, upon the dairymaid's skill in summer depended the winter supplies of butter and cheese for a lot of people. Nowadays in most areas the milk is taken down daily by lorry to central dairies, and anyway the whole system of winter feeding has been reorganised. As a result milk yield has increased while the number of cows has much decreased. The hard monastic existence of the dairymaid is no more. Many an old *seter* is abandoned, and many have become holiday chalets for townsmen.

The greater part of Maihaugen's exhibition hall is laid out in a series of small nineteenth-century country workshops, fully equipped with contemporary tools and examples of half-finished and completed work. Among the crafts represented are a shoemaker, gunsmith, smithy, saddler, furrier, tailor and hatter, an umbrella workshop, a bookbinder, a pipemaker, a silversmith, a watchmaker and a photographer's studio. There are separate displays of sledges, travelling boxes, agricultural tools, silver, ceramics, and so on. There are also changing exhibitions of contemporary craftsmanship. Several hours are needed to give this building the attention it deserves.

One further word on Maihaugen. The detailed English guide-book, though comparatively expensive (Kr10), is essential for obtaining good value from the place. It is full of nuggets of historical and social information, useless but fascinating.

Lillehammer provides other things to do and see: the chair-lift up the mountain, walking, angling, swimming and boating, rock carvings 4 miles away to the north, a power station, and much interesting country. One of Norway's great writers lived on the edge of the town, Sigrid Undset (1882–1949; Nobel Prize 1928). Her historical novels set in thirteenth-century Norway, and her modern novels treating of the problems of women in society, earned her a world-wide reputation.

Another writer and Nobel Prize winner, Bjørnstjerne Bjørnson (1832–1910) lived for many years 11 miles off at Aulestad, which is on route 255 to the north-east of the town. His farm is a museum open to the public. Bjørnson was a great national figure in his own lifetime: poet, novelist, playwright, theatre director, patriot, orator, journalist and publicist. T. K. Derry (*A Short History of Norway*, 187–8) writes: 'it is hard to understand modern Norway unless one takes into account that Bjørnson—the artist in politics, the idealist plunging light-heartedly into public affairs—still has only one rival in the national affections, namely Nansen'.

But we had to leave Lillehammer with these matters untasted. We paused to look at the early stone church of St Olaf's, Ringsaker (twelfth century, enlarged in the thirteenth century). It is worth looking at, especially for a beautiful and intricately carved altar screen. The key is to be had from the parsonage, a long white house near the shore of Lake Mjøsa. Then we motored south down the E6 and spent the night on the outskirts of Hamar.

Hamar dates from the twelfth century. There is a Lutheran cathedral of 1866; there are the ruins of the fine old Catholic cathedral (the bishopric was founded by an Englishman, Nicholas Breakspeare, who went on to become the only English Pope, Adrian IV); there is a railway museum, and here (or farther south at Minnesund) you can board the paddle-steamer, twice sunk and twice raised, already mentioned (page 128), for a leisurely sail to Lillehammer.

But it was time to reach Oslo. It was 20 August and there were not so many days left for us. The quickest route is straight down the E6, but this was full of traffic, so we chose route 24, that runs more or less parallel on the east. This road was a mixture of good and wavy tar and of reasonable gravel. It goes through pretty country, rolling hills, partly farmed, partly thick forest (with a lot of road signs warning of elk, though never a beast to be seen).

At Skarnes we crossed route 2, which leads east to the old fortress town of Kongsvinger and the Swedish frontier, and followed route 175 down the left bank of the Glomma. I had wanted to see something of this long river nearer its mouth, for it is the greatest of the log floatways of Norway, and at its exit through Sarpsborg and Fredrikstad has had developed along its banks a complex of industries dependent on timber (sawmills, pulp and paper factories, etc). Sure enough there were a few logs floating lazily down on the intensely blue water and both banks were lined with a floating barrier of logs chained end to end. This prevents jams accumulating in the bays and tributary streams.

In 1973 we visited Fredrikstad and Sarpsborg. At Sarpsborg the Glomma drops 64ft in falls that may once have been romantically impressive, but which are now cribbed and confined by concrete and entirely dwarfed by factory walls and hydro-electric plant. Even at Fredrikstad the river has not the impressive breadth that we enjoyed farther north on this first visit.

But Fredrikstad is worth a visit for other reasons. The old town, Gamlebyen, built within the preserved ramparts of the seventeenth-century fortress, is an architectural gem, with mainly eighteenth-century wooden houses, cobbled streets, an impressive church, red brick barracks of 1783 that are very fine, a moat still filled with water and crossed by a drawbridge, and a peaceful river-bank walk from which to view the traffic on the Glomma. Amongst much other industry, Fredrikstad builds ships. It is one of the largest shipbuilding centres in Norway, comparable with Oslo and Bergen.

And close by, along that section of route 110 between Fredrikstad and Skjeberg which has been called the Highway of the Ancients, there are concentrated more rock carvings (*plate 30*), stone circles, graves, barrows, mounds and other relics of prehistoric man than we had come across anywhere else in Norway. The *Turistsenter* for Fredrikstad, which is at the eastern end of the great Fredrikstad Bru over the Glomma, has informative leaflets on Gamlebyen, the Highway of the Ancients and other delights of the area. Indeed the province of Østfold is as interesting and beautiful in its way as any in Norway, and is usually neglected by English-speaking visitors.

But to get back to our 1972 track. At Arnes we crossed to the right bank of the Glomma and followed route 173, and from the map picked the little side road to Udenes church for a picnic lunch. This proved to be a winner. The church is isolated on a steep bluff above a sweeping curve of the river, with cornfields and woods running down to the shore. The corn was golden, the woods a rich green. Sitting on a bench in the churchyard munching bread and pâté, we stared and stared. The Glomma here is a considerable river, dropping gently and flowing smoothly, a matronly river in a mature valley.

The white church with its steeple, a landmark for miles about, was closed. The largest memorial in the churchard, as in most others, is to the men who died between 1804 and 1814, in the Napoleonic Wars. To simplify a confusing complication of events, the Norwegians, who were then under Danish control, were dragged into the war when Denmark sided with Napoleon. At some point Denmark-Norway declared war on Sweden, a traditional enemy. A number of minor skirmishes occurred as Swedish forces invaded Norway and were driven back. Then Sweden, after intricate diplomatic and military manoeuvring, became allies of the Russians and English; and since the Russians had appropriated Finland, a Swedish province, Sweden was promised sovereignty over Norway. This was ratified by the Treaty of Kiel in 1814.

The Norwegians had been as stirred as any other people by the release of new ideas that followed the gaining of independence by the former American colonies of the British, and from the French Revolution. They wanted freedom from both Denmark and Sweden. By 1814 the wish for independence had reached into most corners of the country and the people were infuriated at being shuttled without consultation from one rule to another. Before the Swedes could establish their power, the Norwegians declared their independence and elected 112 representatives who met at Eidsvoll, and on 17 May 1814 drew up a constitution. They then set about resisting the Swedes and trying to sell their case to the Allies.

Unfortunately the Allies had been fighting revolutions for twenty years. They were in a conservative frame of mind, disinclined to upset treaties so recently signed. After eight days of resistance to the Swedish armies, the Norwegians had to give way. But they had won a partial victory, for they kept their constitution more or less intact, and the merger between the two countries became a union of crowns rather than a conquest of one people by another. The Norwegians were granted full control over internal affairs. The union lasted until 1905. So it is 17 May that is the national day, a public holiday; and it is 1814, not 1905, that is the great year in Norwegian history.

Eidsvoll is a manor house. It was the home of Karsten Anker, patriot, member of a leading merchant family with large interests in timber, and owner of the nearby (now disused) ironworks. The building has been preserved and is open to the public. It lies just off the E6 about 6 miles below the southern tip of Lake Mjøsa.

From Udenes we moved on route 173 to Sennerud, on the other bank, and then along route 172 to Fetsund. There were larger farms here, and larger fields, mostly arable. Combine-harvesters were cutting barley. We had not seen combine-harvesters in Norway before; the fields and farms had been far too small. But we had now entered the greatest area of fertile land, the lowlands round Oslo fjord, 'tracts of country that emerged from the post-glacial seas enriched with a skin of fertile marine deposits' (Mill, 159).

At Fetsund we found what I had been looking for, a collecting point for the logs (*plate 19*). Beyond Fetsund the Glomma flows through Lake Øyeren. A succession of posts joined by chained logs guide the descending wood into the collecting area. The chain stretches diagonally across the river. As we passed there were many, many hundreds of smallish logs floating in the water, all of course stripped of bark and trimmed of side branches before being committed to their swim.

Forests cover nearly a quarter of the land area of Norway. Contrast this with the 3·1 per cent classed as agricultural land. Thus forest is important for the economy, though not so important as in Finland (71 per cent of the land area) and Sweden (55 per cent). The forests of Norway in fact form a ragged western edge to a great continuous band of coniferous forest that stretches across northern Europe and Asia to the Pacific. Only 17 per cent of Norwegian forest is state-owned. Over half the forest is split in small patches among some 100,000 farmers. As a consequence the exploitation of the forest, despite the growth of co-operatives, cannot easily be organised centrally and on the most economic scale, whereas in Sweden and Finland large private companies and the state operate over vast areas.

Again in contrast to the flat lands of Finland and the rolling hills of Sweden, Norway's mountains make the extraction of timber difficult. Until recently the felling of trees tended to be a winter job, both because there is little work on the farms in winter, and because it is easier to move logs over snow to the rivers (a man, a horse and a sledge still do this in places). Almost all timber was floated down rivers to collecting centres near the heads of fjords. Forest that was not within easy reach of a suitable river was not cut. Now thousands of miles of forest road have been constructed (and, where not closed to the public, are splendid for private camping). Although every big river still floats some timber, road transport by tractor and then by lorry is increasingly used, reaching into areas that used to be inaccessible, and can be carried on through the summer. Floated logs dropped steadily from 40,000 in 1957 to 8,000 in 1970. Mechanisation has changed all aspects of forestry work (one example: power-saws in 1939, nil; in 1969, 100,000), and in a generation has increased output while reducing manpower by two-thirds.

Norway has been exporting timber from the southern districts for centuries: for house-building, shipbuilding, and other domestic uses. Much of Renaissance Amsterdam was built with Norwegian wood, and large quantities were shipped to London after the Great Fire of 1666. Indeed the timber export trade used to affect the prosperity of the whole of the south of the country.

Since the beginning of the present century, however, something so simple as chopping down your trees and exporting them as logs or planks has been pushed aside by a succession of unlikely complications. Trees are now turned into woodpulp, paper (*plate 18*), cardboard, wallboard, cellulose, rayon fibres, alcohol, paint solvent, anti-freeze liquids, wallpaper paste and dozens of other products at the third, fourth and tenth remove from the original plant, and far more profitable. There is now scarcely any export of sawn timber, which is used for home consumption. As with every other industrial development, hydro-electricity has provided the cheap home-produced power to fuel the revolution.

11 Oslo

Strange streets and thick traffic are bewildering to travellers in from forty days in the wilderness. The first few hours of driving in a new city are always tense. City traffic has its own conventions, develops its own personality, to which the foreigner must become attuned. The strain of finding the way from maps that require a magnifying-glass to decipher through such booby-traps as one-way streets, tram lines, traffic lights in unusual positions, policemen at unexpected junctions, sudden spurts of pedestrians, wobbling bicycles, and roads under repair, is so great that tempers are shredded. Oslo has both trams and electric buses, and about half the city centre seemed to be dug up.

Cities are difficult for the camper and motorcaravanner. The time-limit on parking meters means constant movement (and expense); if the van is left outside the metered areas, there is no fixed base in which to recuperate from the exhaustion of shopping, museum slogging, and walking on crowded pavements. The streets of every European city in summer are awash with haggard faces and aching feet.

In Oslo parking meters are of three types: yellow—maximum parking time one hour; grey—parking time two hours; and green—parking time four hours. In the centre most meters are yellow. The information bureau has a useful coloured map that shows which type of meters are where; also a short free guide to the city, and a weekly publication called *Oslo This Week*.

At the accommodation bureau inside the East Station, for a booking fee of Kr8, we were fixed up over the phone with a room in a third-floor flat of a large nineteenth-century house in the residential district midway between Slottsparken and Frognerparken.

We thought it would be good to live in a house for two or three nights, to have baths, to relax on a comfortable bed.

It did not work out that way. There were trams and traffic until a late hour and again from about 5.30 am. Aircraft, which we had forgotten, passed low overhead gaining height. There was a neurotic magpie at dawn cackling interminably. And the mattress was hard. Our hostess spoke English; she was not unfriendly, but not curious, perhaps shy. Once she had given us a key to the front door of house and flat, we did not communicate, which was a pity.

There were two things we had to do in Oslo. One was to visit the Munch museum; the other was to see the viking ships. The ships are a 'must' for everyone interested in the viking achievement; and Edvard Munch (1863–1944) is one of the most extraordinary painters of our age (*plate 24*).

Munch bequeathed an immense number of oil paintings, water-colours, drawings, etchings, lithographs, woodcuts and sculptures to the city of Oslo, to which other works have since been added. The museum built specially for them was opened in 1963. There are over 20,000 items; only a small proportion can be shown. The museum is free, but note that it is closed on Mondays and on Sunday mornings.

Munch is not too well known in England or America. This is perhaps because few of his paintings have been available for purchase to galleries outside Oslo. You have to go to Oslo to appreciate the volume and the varied content of his work. Munch is called an 'Expressionist'. But labels often hide more than they explain. He painted what he felt as much as what he saw. By means of simplification, distortion, sometimes by exaggeration, he tried to express a spiritual mood or condition, to show emotion, to reveal inner states of mind. He 'bends and forces nature and his model beneath the influence of mood, and changes them in order to get more out of them' (Christian Krohg, quoted by Hodin, 50). If this sounds forbidding, I can only beg the visitor to spend an hour in the Munch museum. It will be a revelation. The later works are perhaps more immediately likeable, often lyrical, less violent. But those painted before his breakdown in 1908 have a power and depth and fascination that are hard to resist.

There is work by Munch elsewhere in Oslo: in the National Gallery, in the Assembly Hall of the University (a set of magnificent and important murals), and in the Freia chocolate factory (more murals). On the west coast of Oslo fjord, at Åsgårdstrand, is the house which Munch bought in 1897 and owned until his death, though he did not live there much in later years. This house is open to the public. The scenery around Åsgårdstrand and its beach appears in many of Munch's pictures.

To the west of Oslo on the Bygdøy peninsula, among the expensive houses, the yachting marinas and the remaining fields, is scattered a series of museums. Among these is the building that houses the three viking ships from Oseberg, Gokstad and Tune, together with many of the equally remarkable objects discovered at the sites. If we knew nothing of viking art but what is shown in this museum, we should still rate it very high. The building itself has a notable interior: four white tunnels radiating like the arms of a cross from a central space. In three of them are the ships, long, powerful, elegant; in the fourth are the other finds.

By the middle of the eighth century the viking sailing-ship had been perfected, a product of centuries of experiment and development while sailing among the leads and fjords, the gulfs and sounds and belts and archipelagoes, the rivers and lakes of the Scandinavian north. The viking eruption was dependent upon command of the sea. It was skill in shipbuilding and a mastery of navigation beyond that possessed by their neighbours, and not a monopoly of courage, that enabled the Norsemen to appear unheralded before Rouen or London, to ply regularly round the north of Scotland down to Dublin, to cross non-stop to Iceland, to Greenland, to visit North America, to sail the rivers of Russia from the White Sea to the Black, to raid, trade or settle when and where they pleased.

The ocean-striding longship, with its flexible frame, its speed, its shallow draught (allowing it to run in from the sea up rivers or on to beaches), its effective side-rudder, its ability to sail close to the wind, its manoeuvrability, its choice of oar or wind for power, and its disciplined crew, was a most remarkable—and beautiful—instrument for war. Viking ships were the finest of their age; the master-shipbuilders who made them enjoyed high status.

The three grave-ships in the museum are not the only ones to have been recovered; nor are they representative of the variety of boat that was then available, with the major divisions between merchantmen (high, short and broad-beamed) and warships (low, long and narrow), and between coastal and sea-going vessels. But they are certainly the most complete. You will not find anything like them elsewhere.

Until the arrival of Christianity in the eleventh century, there was much variety in the treatment of the dead: some were buried, some cremated; some would be accompanied by an abundance of objects (clothing, jewellery, weapons, coins, tools, food, bodies of horses, dogs, even people), some would be buried with few goods or none; some graves are marked by mounds of varying size, some by cairns, some by circles or other patterns of stones, some went unmarked. It is the ship burials that are the most spectacular, and a great many hundreds have been found in Norway alone, though often the ship is only a small boat. Sometimes the ship is represented symbolically, by stones arranged in the shape of a boat. Whether this expenditure of labour and wealth is designed as a send-off into the next world, or whether the dead were thought to 'live' in their graves—and both beliefs and others seem to have existed—we have them to thank for our possession of many beautiful objects. We would have more if most graves had not been looted.

Viking skill in shaping and carving wood is fully displayed in the ship museum. Viking craftsmanship in metal and jewellery can be seen in the Historical Museum at the university (opening times

Page 143 (above) 28 *mountains and fjords near the Arctic Circle;* (below) 29 *Eidsborg stave church (page 162). Detail of the west porch showing the sheath of overlapping wood tiles, each hand-carved, and the much older carved columns on either side of the door*

Page 144 (above) 30 *detail from the rock carvings at Begby, near Fredrikstad, on the Highway of the Ancients (page 134). These are a few inches high and only a small part of the total number to be seen on this site alone;* (below left) 31 *Leirfall rock carvings, Hegra, near Trondheim (page 67), showing some of the stylised ships of the 'farmers' art;* (below right) 32 *the Narvik reindeer, a true example of the prehistoric naturalistic hunters' art (pages 68,86)*

vary according to the day and month). In its treasure room are gathered most of the gold and silver objects found in south-eastern Norway during the viking age and the centuries before and after, and very beautiful some of them are. (Similar museums at Bergen, Trondheim, Tromsø and Stavanger cater for the other areas of the country).

The Oslo Historical Museum covers all periods between the Old Stone Age and the Middle Ages. It has a splendid collection of carved doorways and carved figures from demolished stave churches, and for these alone you should try to visit it. One room supports a marvellous painted ceiling from the vanished *stavkirke* at Ål in the Hallingdal.

On a south-east spur of that same Bygdøy peninsula are three other ship museums. All can be reached easily by car or bus, or by ferry across the harbour from the piers at Rådhusplassen, the open space and water-front before Rådhuset, the city hall.

The Kon-Tiki Museum houses Thor Heyerdahl's balsawood raft, *Kontiki*, on which he and five others drifted westwards across the Pacific from Peru in 1947. There are also exhibits from Easter Island, and of Heyerdahl's more recent voyage across the Atlantic on the papyrus boat, *Raa*. *Raa* itself has been preserved and in 1973 was on temporary display elsewhere in the city.

Close by are two rather beautiful buildings like vast ridge tents. One is the Boat Hall of the Maritime Museum, housing exhibits of boats used round the coasts of Norway, models of sailing ships, and much else. The other holds Fridtjof Nansen's polar exploration ship, *Fram*. This boat was also used in 1910–11 to carry Roald Amundsen to the Antarctic, where he forestalled Scott as the first man to reach the South Pole.

Nansen (1861–1930) and Amundsen (1872–1928) each led several polar expeditions and contributed widely to scientific knowledge. But Nansen achieved more. In 1905, armed with his own international reputation as an explorer and scientist, and not a great deal

I

else, he did as much as anyone to enlighten opinion in Europe as to the justice and seriousness of Norway's reach for independence from Sweden. In 1922 he gained the Nobel Peace Prize for his work in feeding and rehabilitating millions of refugees in Europe and Asia created by World War I. In the League of Nations he was a spokesman for the small nations of the world. His influence was extraordinary. He was a great European as well as a great Norwegian. The measure of Nansen's popularity in Norway can be judged by the number of statues of him that populate the squares, parks and other public spaces. The semicircular space to the north of Rådhuset is called Fridtjof Nansens plass.

Rådhuset is a dominating building, and a controversial one both inside and out (*plate 22*). It was built between 1931 and 1950. The entrance is on the side away from the harbour, and is lined with painted wooden reliefs by Dagfin Werenskiold of scenes from Norse mythology. Inside the main hall marble abounds and the walls are covered with vast murals by various hands. The total effect is colourful, but in detail the paintings demonstrate one marked facet of Norwegian 'official' art: a tendency to depict groups of solemn workers in cloth caps, while in the background solemn wives and their healthy children display their solidarity in more than one sense.

The area round Rådhuset is thick with statues. Among them are fine specimens of the ubiquitous nude maiden (*plate 25*). Presumably these stalwart ladies symbolise fertility, yet despite their curves they seem neuter.

The apogee of sculptural display in Oslo is, of course, the Frognerparken, or Vigeland Park. It is a large and beautiful park, with a lake, fountains, waterfalls, flower beds, grass and trees, and an open-air swimming pool in one corner. But the chief attraction must be the 150 sculptural groups by Gustav Vigeland (1869–1943). These are even more controversial than Rådhuset. Vigeland is Norway's greatest sculptor, or at least the most prolific, comparable to Munch, and living through the same period. The story of his creations in this park and the bargain he made with the city of Oslo is told in every guidebook.

My own reaction to this extraordinary display of one man's prodigal creativity is divided. Vigeland's children, teenagers and old people seemed to me mostly good, but his adults wooden, especially the flat headed, over-muscled, Teutonic men. Some viewers regard the whole thing as a sick nightmare. Yet it is impertinent to make quick judgements on a lifetime's work that reveals such will-power and energy and talent: anyone who has tried to create anything must remain a little humble before it. And I have been told that one should not criticise his work without seeing the nearby Vigeland Museum, once his studio, which contains a further 1,650 sculptures, 3,700 woodcuts, 11,000 sketches.

The open-air folk museum on the Bygdøy peninsula is of the same breed as the Sandvig Collections at Maihaugen (page 128), though not in such pretty grounds. It is at once better and worse. It is better because its 150 wooden buildings are from most districts from Trøndelag southwards. It is worse in that many of them are not furnished, or are sparsely furnished. Thus one can study a greater variety of rural architecture, but cannot obtain that vivid impression of how life used to be lived that is given at Maihaugen. Some of the houses in the 'old town' are fully furnished, and in fact this is an interesting corner because elsewhere in Norway these open-air museums can seldom include town houses.

The *stavkirke* from Gol in Hallingdal which was re-erected here is fairly heavily restored, but restored with sense, so that it probably does resemble the original twelfth-century building, and not some romantic hybrid of the restorer's imagination. There is a good catalogue in English.

Some visitors may prefer the exhibition rooms round the great entrance courtyard (not listed in the catalogue). These mostly contain furnished rooms from town houses in Oslo and its neighbourhood, but only a proportion of the items are Norwegian—the greater part are imports from Holland, France, England, etc. The folk museum also contains a Lapp section, and Henrik Ibsen's study, which is dark (as no doubt it was) and out of bounds, so not much can be seen as one peers through the door.

Oslo looks its best from a distance, when its setting of hills and fjords redeems it, like pretty hair round a plain face. One vantage point from which to view it is the ski jump at Holmenkollen. A landmark from almost anywhere, it is worth visiting both for the view and for itself. It is reached by road, or gently up the mountain railway, the Holmenkollen line, from the National Theatre underground station in Karl Johans gate. For the best views, get seats on the left-hand side of the train as you face the front. There is a lift up most of the tower that supports the ski jump, and a closed-in observation platform at the top (1,351ft above sea level). The lift remains open until 10 pm. It is as good to ascend after dark as in daylight, for the lights of the city spread round the harbour in a glittering semicircle, and climb the hills, and bedizen the islands; and across the water fishing boats* and liners burn and sparkle their individual tracks.

From the top also there is the skier's stomach-turning view down the slope of the jump. In summer it ends in a lake. This jump is for the experts; the world championships were held here in 1966. The national competition in March each year is one of Oslo's major events. All over Norway there are local competitions from smaller jumps, often rickety-looking structures of wooden scaffolding that seem a little absurd stuck among the trees and grass of a summer hillside.

Tucked underneath the Holmenkollen jump is a ski museum that traces the evolution of the ski from an example that is 2,500 years old through to modern times.

From higher up the same hill, where the railway ends at Frogner-seteren, there are miles of walks along paths among woods and lakes that all belong to the city and can never be built over. In winter the

* Fishing for brisling (sprats) is done at night with the aid of powerful batteries of lights mounted on a frame and towed in another boat behind.

paths become ski trails, and from some the darkness of the winter afternoons and evenings is banished by overhead lights. Skiing is second nature to most Norwegians, and cross-country skiing almost a way of life for many.

Although Oslo is at the head of a fjord, one has to go some few miles down one side or the other for sea bathing. The water near the city is too polluted by the docks, factories and shops and the 193,000 houses. Even down the coast—say at Ingjerstrand, which is a nice place to bathe—the usual clarity of Norway's sea is missing. This is partly because the inner reaches of Oslofjorden have little tide—about 10 inches—since the exit through Vestfjorden is narrow; and partly because the influx of treated sewage and other matter, though safe, encourages the growth of algae that cloud the sea.

A visitor could overcome this by motoring to the area of Moss and Jeløy island (34 miles on the E6) on the east side, or to the Tofte or Holmestrand coastline on the west. Or you might take the hydrofoil ferry from Rådhusplassen to Tofte or Horten (1¼ hours).* There is a car ferry from Horten to Moss, so it would be feasible to plan a round trip. And this would make sense as a piece of historical, economic and geographical exploration, for Oslo's growth to pre-eminence depends in part upon its location at the apex of the two counties that line Oslofjorden: Østfold and Vestfold.

These provinces contain Norway's largest concentration of good farmland (Trøndelag and the district south of Stavanger are the other two important areas) and its greatest concentration of industry. They form the heart of the country today. Indeed Vestfold was the home of the first kings of Norway and saw the growth of the oldest existing towns. And earlier in prehistory both sides of the fjord were host to a succession of cultures.

Oslo is said to have been founded around 1048 by Harald Hadråde, the buccaneering Harald who was killed in England in 1066 at the battle of Stamford Bridge. But the town remained of minor importance until (a) Haakon V decided to move his capital from

* Just south of Horten is Borre where, in a national park, are 'the greatest number of royal burial mounds in N. Europe'.

Trondheim, and built the citadel of Akershus in about 1300; (b) in
1380 political control over Norway passed to Denmark and the
centre of power to Copenhagen, with Oslo closer to hand; and (c)
the Hansa in Bergen killed much of Trondheim's trade in that same
century.

Despite these factors and possession of one of Europe's finest
natural harbours, and although it was the seat of a real government
after the union with Sweden in 1814, Oslo stayed a small town until
near the close of the nineteenth century. It seems to have been the
introduction of free trade in the 1870s, the building of the telegraph
network during the same period (enabling nationwide business to be
undertaken cheaply and quickly), and above all the expansion of the
railways in this century that caused the final breakthrough. Here are
some population figures: 1624, 3,000; 1800, 12,000; 1840, 20,000;
1900, 228,000; 1948, 348,000; 1971, 482,000. At under half a million
Oslo is still a small city. And it is still an immigrant city, with a high
proportion of its citizens born elsewhere.

Railways opened up the interior of Norway just as earlier they
had opened up Canada and the United States. Especially they carried
fresh life to the great valleys that converge, like the spokes of a wheel,
on Oslo fjord (though not on Oslo) from the north: Østerdalen,
Gudbrandsdalen, the Valdres, Hallingdalen (which cossets the early
sections of the magnificent Bergensbanen) and Numedalen. As well
as these valley lines, the Sørland railway, with branches, links Oslo
to Stavanger, 372 miles to the west. And there are lines joining Oslo
to Gøteborg and Stockholm in Sweden.

Most of this mileage was built in the twentieth century, much of it
in the last fifty years at a time when railways in other countries have
been in decline. Norway's railways have served a political as well
as an economic and social purpose, drawing the nation together as
perhaps nothing else could have done, and bringing once remote
areas into easy communication with the capital. Bergen and
Trondheim face the Atlantic; Oslo is closer to the Baltic world. It
needed the railways (assisted now by the aeroplane) to overcome the
centrifugal tendencies of such diverse regions.

Oslo is more than the political and cultural capital; from the beginnings of Norway's industrialisation in the 1840s it has been the largest industrial centre. Textiles, shipbuilding, iron and steel plants, engineering works, printing presses, flour mills, and many other local enterprises employ over a quarter of the country's industrial workers.

Very little of Oslo is old. It was burned down in 1624 and rebuilt on a new site by Christian IV, that most active of the Danish kings of Norway. Parts of it were burned again later, most disastrously in 1858. Akershus Castle on its rock by the harbour—enlarged and restored and the object of several sieges—dates from the late thirteenth century. The Gamle Aker Church at the northern end of Akersveien, built about 1100, though also much restored, is one of the few early stone churches in Norway to have survived in more or less its original shape. It resembles both in plan and date, and in its severity of style, the church at Ringsaker (page 133). Not much else can claim the sanctity of age.

It is sad for modern Oslo that so much of it was built during the middle and late nineteenth century, an unimaginative period in architecture and city planning. Where are the pleasing vistas of blue fjord that could and should have been engineered after the 1858 fire? There are none. The views to the sea are mostly blocked, and the waterfront everywhere is a mess of docks. The only section that is 'public'—the piers in front of Rådhuset—is divided from the city by a fierce flow of traffic and, when reached, proves unromantically dull: no trees, no cafés, no strings of lamps to glitter in the water at night, nothing to attract anybody but the ferries that can take them somewhere else (*plate 22*).

The central streets are dull. Nineteenth-century civic and commerical architecture was solid, safe and respectable, hardly ever interesting, amusing, inspiring or lovable. The connoisseur of nineteenth-century styles will no doubt find things to enjoy: perhaps in the Slottet, the Royal Palace (1848); in the central university buildings (1851–4); maybe even in the Storting, or parliament house (1866)—all in Karl Johans gate. The Domkirke, the

cathedral, dates from 1694 with later embellishments and restora-
tions. In my limited viewing it is in some of the inner western
suburbs, where the prohibition on the use of wood did not prevail,
that one comes across patches of attractive private houses. And
scattered elsewhere are good examples of modern building (flats,
houses, schools, and so on) some of which have made imaginative
use of hill-sites overlooking the city and fjord (*plate 23*).

Oslo has colder winters than Bergen and Trondheim. In 1968 it
had 163 days of frost, while Bergen had 82 and Trondheim 142.
But it is drier than either. There is a lot of sun in winter. The recent
rapid increase in the city's population has brought a housing
shortage. The cost of living is high, as everywhere in Norway, and is
rising. A country so dependent on imports for its food and industry
is at the mercy of conditions elsewhere that it cannot control, and
there is a world shortage of many basic raw materials.

Yet despite these and other disadvantages, I think Oslo is a city
one could grow to like living in. It may not be beautiful or grand,
but it is comprehensible, still on a human scale. It is penetrated by the
sea and the countryside to a degree that few other capitals can rival;
cities are for people, and people need a change from streets.

12 Vestfold, Telemark, Kristiansand

Our camp was a clearing in the woods at the end of a forest track. The track was a few hundred feet up on a ridge west of Sande, which is south of Drammen. The valleys here are cultivated, the ridges covered with forest.

After the city it was good to be back in the van and in quiet surroundings; so good that we lingered in our private world all next morning. No one on the whole over-populated globe knew that we were there—a sobering thought.

On top of a 15ft bank behind the clearing we found droppings that were far too large for sheep, and were unlike any other in our repertoire. So they were named 'possibly elk'. We hoped to see their former owner round every bush. Unlike reindeer, elk are solitary animals; they like forests, and still live in fair numbers in southern Norway.

Later, stalking quietly through the woods in the hope of a glimpse of an ear or a tail, or at least of some animal life, we did come on a black woodpecker making an enormous noise as it hacked long strips of wood about 3ft from the base of a dead conifer. It was the first bird we had seen that cannot be found somewhere in the British Isles.

This camp was a suntrap and perfectly peaceful. If only I had been able to subdue an ambition to see a good stretch more of

Norway in our remaining few days, we could have stayed for a second night. But we picked a supply of bilberries and left at 1 pm. The plan was to sample the south coast around Stavern and the Brunlanes peninsula; then to raid north into the province of Telemark, and finally to come south again through the Setesdal to Kristiansand, from where we were booked to sail on 30 August.

Stavern, at the southern end of route 301 from Larvik, is a sleepy sort of place of wooden houses, trees, benches to doze on, and water. It must once have been brisker, but now carries a faded aristocratic air. The old fortress of Frederiksvern (1750–6) protected a naval base that would have been busy enough during the Napoleonic Wars and other times of crisis. The fortress is now an air force training centre, but the public can walk through at certain hours to a rocky peninsula beyond, which is a good place to bathe. Inside the turf-covered ramparts are great red warehouse buildings from the 1790s, and yellow-painted living quarters. The sentries look bored.

Outside Stavern on another peninsula is a hideous pyramid of a monument, the Minnehallen, to the seamen who lost their lives in the two world wars. From the platform there is a nice view of Stavern and the surrounding skerries. In the chamber below, where an elderly guardian immured in gloom demanded our signatures and a krone or two, are the names of the dead on brass plaques, and of the ships sunk. It is a reminder that though Norway was neutral in the 1914–18 war, she lost 2,000 lives and half her merchant navy, a tonnage greater than that of any combatant nation except Britain. Again, in World War II, half her merchant tonnage was lost, and some 3,600 lives.

We spent that night in a field beside an inlet of the sea. It was an unlisted camp site somewhere near Berg, with one other tent, earth lavatories, and a couple of taps in the open. The setting sun glinted across the water, and as the receding tide exposed mud banks farther out, sea birds gathered in hundreds. The field was part of a working farm; tractors were busy until it was too dark to see.

A bonus from any holiday is the unexpected, which can be as pleasing in small ways as in large. We woke to a thick mist, and lay in bed listening to three foghorns blaring mournfully in different tones somewhere out in the Skagerak. There were seagulls crying in an extraordinary variety of voices, from a parrot-like screech to a deep caw. Across the stretch of still water close beside us an old man rowed by, out of the mist and into it. Then there was no one in view, no one at all.

The farmer at the camp refused to take our money, another bonus. Moreover his wife gave us a bag of fresh carrots, harvested, cleaned and packed on the farm. There are acres of onions and carrots growing down here.

The next objective was the burial mounds at Mølen. These are on the shore at the edge of a peninsula between the fishing ports of Helgeroa and Nevlunghavn. There are no signposts and it took us nearly an hour of pursuing false trails before we found them. They are made of heaped boulders. Just here the surface of the earth is all rock, boulders and round stones, for this is where a massive moraine that crosses the Brunlanes peninsula, Vestfoldraet, hits the sea. For the length of the south-eastern shore of Norway, or just off-shore, the Finiglacial stage (about 8000 BC) of the Quaternary Ice Age rested on a more or less stationary line for 800 years, and left behind it enormous quantities of debris.

In the literature these burial mounds, now about 15ft high and 60–100ft in diameter, are said to be Bronze Age. But a young archaeologist at work near one of them said they were later, about AD 400–600. The large mounds seem to be enclosed by two or more lines of very small mounds.

The outer coast of the Brunlanes peninsula from Nevlunghavn to Stavern has a number of good beaches, coves and camping sites. Indeed Sørlandet, the whole coastline of southern Norway and its hinterland, can offer much to those who want lazing, bathing, sailing and fishing. It is a coastline of low skerries, narrow sounds, twisting inlets and unspoilt, wooden towns. We touched only the fringe, here and at Kristiansand, but we met others who knew it well and were enthusiastic. It is an area which is greatly favoured by the people of Oslo. Spring comes sooner, autumn later, and it can often be hot. In July and August the sea is said to be the warmest in Europe after the Mediterranean.

In the late afternoon we motored through Larvik and north up route 8 and the Lågen valley for Kongsberg. There had been rain, but this had stopped and a bright slanting sun made the valley enchanting: great wooded spurs, golden corn, brilliant green grass, white and red farms, and the river glass-clear. The Lågen river is said to be full of salmon in season (1 May to 12 September). Norway is salmon country, though fishing on the best reaches is expensive. Fishing for other species can be cheap; in fact sea fishing is free. (A multilingual leaflet published by the Norwegian Travel Association gives details.)

Kongsberg (the king's mountain), which we entered next morning, is an interesting town. It can be reached in not much over an hour on the direct route from Oslo. It was founded in 1624 by the order of Christian IV when silver was discovered in the neighbourhood. This is the same energetic Christian who rebuilt Oslo after the fire of 1624, who founded Kristiansand, and who encouraged the growth of Røros after the discovery of copper there in 1644 (page 119). He also founded iron mines in many parts of the country. Around 1770 Kongsberg employed 4,000 miners and was the second largest city in the country. It declined as the output of silver fell. Its chief activities now are an arms factory, tourists, and the mint; it is a developing winter-sports centre.

As with Røros and its copper, the most obvious physical legacy of the silver days in Kongsberg is the church, a fine eighteenth-century rococo building set in the older part of the town. The exterior is plain brick, with a pretty copper cupola on a brick tower. The interior is a surprise: a huge place with three tiers of galleries, an elaborately painted ceiling and, in the centre of the west side, one above the other, the altar, pulpit, a balcony for the choir, and the organ. This unusual grouping is rich with carving and colour, mainly gold and blue. Everything is in wood, however much it resembles marble. Along the east wall are the king's box and two tiers of lesser boxes, as in a theatre. Hanging from the ceiling are three superb chandeliers made at the Nøstetangen Glassworks.*

The silver mines, 4 miles out, were closed in 1957. The public is taken on a miniature railway into the mountain to see them. There is also a mining museum in the town, for the Kongsberg mines were central to the development of mining in Norway.

We left in the early afternoon, taking route 8 north up the Numedal, but soon turning west along route 37, a beautiful, hilly road through woods and past lakes, rivers and a few farms. This is the eastern edge of Telemark, the county that is said to contain the most elaborate *stabbur* (page 130). We saw nice examples of the plainer variety, but one needs time and more information to seek out the best.

From the northern tip of Lake Tinnsjø a number of secondary roads penetrate up the eastern rim of the Hardangervidda. For a walk on the plateau we were advised to try the road which climbs the Gausetdal. It was narrow, twisting, never level and often spectacular, and it took half an hour of steady grinding in second and third gear before we found a place to drive off for the night.

Next morning after another half hour we reached Kalhovd, well above the tree line. Kalhovd turned out to be a few houses at the head of a dam. The only human to appear was a drunk, who kept demanding schnapps. We pretended not to understand. Soon he got tired of watching us pull on socks and boots. He slouched away, disappearing into the open landscape as suddenly as a flatfish into sand.

These Hardanger moors are on a big scale. You can see a long way. We walked on a well-worn track going north-west towards Mårbu. Apart from the initial climb from the dam, the gradients were easy. There were ultramarine lakes in every hollow, brilliant

---

* The Nøstetangen Glassworks opened in 1741, and from 1748 concentrated on ornamental glass. It is Norway's most famous glassworks whose pieces are often to be found in museums.

in the sun; there were grey and pink rocks spotted with green
lichen, bilberry bushes (and others) turning orange, scatterings of
white cloud and a cooling north wind. To the south rose Mount
Gausta, 6,178ft.

The Hardangervidda is a plateau of lakes and moorland, of low
ridges and rounded hills, of soft contours. Mostly it lies between
3,000 and 5,000ft, but is higher towards the north and towards the
west where it abuts on to the inner Hardangerfjord. It is the largest
of the Norwegian plateaux, one of Europe's last wildernesses,
crossed by only one road (route 7) and one railway, both towards
the northern edge, and is trackless over many square miles. Once it
was covered with forest. Then glaciers scoured away the fertile soil
and left behind gravel, sand, clay, a jumble of boulders, and bedrock
and lakes. Such moors hold water like a sponge. Plants that die
make peat. Mosses, lichens and heather are everywhere; trees are
absent, birds scarce. There are said to be thousands of reindeer,
though we saw none. The lakes and rivers have fish.

On this bleak upland early man settled in considerable numbers.
The hunting was good. And around Lake Mosvatn, south-west of
Kalhovd, are the remains of many ovens and slag-heaps left from the
extraction of bog-iron in viking times. Iron was vital to the viking
economy, both for weapons and for the tools of an expanding
agriculture.

Route 37 skirts Lake Tinnsjø at its north-west end. Then it turns
into the deep cleft of Vestfjorddalen. In this cleft lies Rjukan, which
is better known than Oslo to many British and Americans because
of the film *The Heroes of Telemark*, about the war-time sabotage
raid by Norwegian commandos on the German-controlled heavy-
water plant at Vemork, just up the valley. Heavy water was essential
for the development of the atomic bomb. The Rjukan falls, a famous
sight for visiting Englishmen of the nineteenth century, have been
emasculated for the needs of electricity.

Rjukan is a good example of the necessary enterprise of Norwegian industry. In this remote corner of Telemark, originally attracted by cheap hydro-electric power, the giant Norsk Hydro manufactures synthetic ammonia. First it used the Birkeland-Eyde process; then the Haber-Bosch technique, and now, to remain competitive, it has changed to oil-based production—three revolutions in half a century. The liquid ammonia is carried by rail in tank wagons to Lake Tinnsjø, where the wagon trains run on to ferries which take them 25 miles to Tinnoset at the southern end. Here they meet another railway that takes them via Notodden to Herøya on the coast near Porsgrunn. At Herøya the ammonia is the principal material used in the production of nitric acid and the manufacture of nitrogenous fertilisers, which are then exported. Norsk Hydro has another synthetic ammonia plant above the Arctic Circle at Glomfjord, close to the great Svartisen icecap (*plate 26*). From here the liquid ammonia is transported in tankers 800 miles to Herøya, year in, year out.

Some of those facets of geography that helped to keep the country backward for centuries have been harnessed and in less than a century have transformed it into a prosperous industrialised nation. Nowadays more people are employed in industry and mining than in all other primary occupations combined; Norway is no longer a nation of farmers and fishermen.

At Rjukan we wanted to visit Mår power station. We nearly failed. It turned out that the season for visitors had closed on 20 August, and that some malfunctioning was engrossing everyone's attention. The entrance to a Norwegian underground power station is usually inconspicuous. At Mår there was a brick office set against the foot of the mountain; there was a rail track that disappeared beneath large doors; and there was a canalised flow of water, the tail-race, sliding out of a tunnel. We were gazing disconsolately at these when a man emerged from the office. He was wearing a tin helmet and carrying a briefcase. Although on his way to reach the bank before it closed, he offered us a quick tour, which was extraordinarily kind.

He was an engineer, not in the station, but concerned with the linked lakes and rivers.

Mår is totally underground. We passed immediately into a large and cold tunnel, about 30ft high and 15ft wide, very clean, white, empty except for a row of lights along the top and the rail-track under foot. Power stations are placed deep inside mountains partly for strategic, but mostly for technical reasons. Norwegians probably lead the world in the techniques for tunnelling through solid rock. They have done so much of it, first with roads and railways, then with power stations. Since the latest equipment makes a comparatively quick job of excavation, the power plant and turbines of a power station can be placed well inside to give a steeper intake fall. Feeder tunnels are drilled through the mountains to reservoirs that may be miles away. Indeed at Mår the source of supply was the lake formed by the dam at Kalhovd, where we had just walked, 15 miles off in a direct line. Whole chains of lakes and rivers can be linked in this way. In northern Europe, going underground gives the added advantage of protection from the winter cold.

At the far end of the access tunnel was a narrow passage through natural rock that led to the foot of the descending twin pipes. The water falling down the pipes hits specially-shaped waterwheels with great force, and the turning of the wheels works the turbines and generators. The latter are in a huge hall. There is no smoke. There is no dirt. Overlooking the hall is the control room, operated by one man. The same man could control four or five linked stations if necessary, and is in touch with stations over much of south-east Norway and parts of Sweden. Mår is operated by 20–25 men. If built today, according to our guide, one or two men would suffice.

We spent a cold night in a stone quarry high above the Rjukan valley on the flanks of Mount Gausta, which has been called the Fujiyama of Norway. The 6,000ft mountain towers 3,000ft above the surrounding plateau, and 5,000ft above Rjukan. We climbed it early the next morning. The climb is not difficult, but is tiring. It took us 2½ hours, with several short breaks, plodding steadily. There is a marked path from a saddle on the Dale-Tuddalsdalen road. The upper part of the mountain is sheathed in close-packed boulders coloured yellow-green with lichen, like the mountain we had climbed in the Rondane. From the top the view is very remark-able: on a clear sunny morning such as we were lucky to have it is said to cover near a sixth of Norway. It is probably the most extensive view that most of us are likely to see with our feet on land. One looks down 5,000ft to the Mår power station, and for 360° over miles and miles of lake-studded plateau to horizons punctuated by snow ranges. The sides of the mountain are scored with large shallow gulleys or rock shutes that stretch from top to bottom and give it a streaked appearance. To look down these from above makes for vertigo.

Unfortunately, near the top of Gausta there is now a tower, possibly a transmitter, apparently clothed in green plastic, and a tourist hut. It took the edge from our achievement to find an elderly couple behind the bar in the hut. Worse was to follow. We had climbed with the mountain to ourselves, assuming that our effort, though requiring no skill, was at least mildly exceptional. We had not been fifteen minutes on the summit ridge when hosts of Norwegians began to arrive. They were of all ages and dressed in every type of clothing. A large party of young girls and boys went leaping past like goats to the true summit at the far end of the ridge, which I later found to be a difficult and slightly hair-raising scramble up and over or round a series of vast chunks of rock. One man went past carrying a dog. Women were arriving in shorts and bras. It began to seem like a bank holiday at an English seaside resort.

But it was a most remarkable view.

We did not return to Rjukan, but drove south from Mount Gausta into the heart of Telemark, one of the least changed counties of Norway. Over 100 years ago Mattieu Williams called it 'the wildest, most barren and dreary of the inhabited regions'. M.W. was on

K

foot, which makes a difference. It is still wild, much of it is still barren, but it is not dreary. One could spend a good few days exploring its valleys and walking its mountains. It was from Telemark that the use of skis for sport spread to Oslo in the nineteenth century, and so to the rest of the world. Unfortunately our time was now limited, and our exploration necessarily brisk.

Motoring westwards along the E76 (another possible route between Oslo and Bergen), we stopped briefly at Seljord to take in ice cream and the church. The church is a delightful early stone building with a dumpy wooden steeple and a wooden porch at the west end (*plate 17*). On the hill behind is a statue to Marcus Brostrup Landstad (1802–80), a famous itinerant preacher who was one of the first to collect and publish the ballads and legends of the Norwegian countryside.

Then at Ofte we turned south-west on to route 45 to cross the mountains to the Setesdal. At Eidsborg, in a beautiful setting, there is a stave church; it was opened for us and for a Norwegian family by an old man who switched from fluent Norwegian to hesitant gentle English without warning or pause. Eidsborg, a late example of the style, was altered and enlarged to the east in the nineteenth century, and restored in the 1920s (*plate 29*). Along the path beyond the church is a small open-air museum of country buildings.

After Eidsborg the road hairpins down the cliffs above Lake Bandak to Dalen. On the north bank of the lake is the Tokke I power station, said to be the largest in northern Europe, and one of a linked group of six with a vast network of feeder waterways. Guided tours can be arranged.

Route 45 (now asphalt) then climbs past lakes and through forests (*plate 21*) over another mountain divide to the Setesdal at Rotemo. The Setesdal valley has been much described and praised for its scenery, its folklore and its distinctive culture. Until quite recent times it was cut off from easy communication with the rest of Norway by its surrounding mountains; thus traditional ways from medieval times survived longer. Commander Stagg has written that at Byglandsfjord, the village at the southern end of the lake of the same name, lies 'one of the most pronounced racial frontiers in all Norway—quite suddenly there is a complete change in racial characteristics, dress, architecture and decoration, language and customs, way of life, cuisine, etc'. (Stagg, 154). Alas, the speeding motorist twisting down the valley road will be sharp-eyed indeed to note any of these differences. The inside of a moving car is not the proper base for anthropological discoveries. But the scenery is certainly splendid.

Commander Stagg also states that it was the heights above Valle and Bykle that for centuries provided the falcons for the kings and courtiers of England and Holland. That I find a fascinating snippet of information.

From Rotemo we turned south towards Kristiansand, and along this section there are first a succession of great rock bluffs and precipices dropping severely to the valley floor, which is flat; then for miles the road twists along the banks of two long lakes. From Evje the road to Kristiansand is new, wide and fast.

The Setesdal is famous for its silver work. According to a notice outside the silversmiths' shop at Helle, the designs are descended from medieval and viking styles. They are of an intricate filigree type which one can admire without in the least wanting to possess. But taste is not yet standardised, and there will be many who like what they see and will want to buy. There is so much emphasis in the tourist literature on the uniqueness of Setesdalen that there is a danger of the whole area becoming a museum, 'quaint'; it may thus lose whatever now survives of its pre-industrial character.

Kristiansand, the end of our exploration, the last call of our voyage, is a town that owes its foundation to a royal command. That indefatigable monarch Christian IV of Denmark needed a fort and port that would protect the southern coast of Norway and command the entrance to the North Sea and the Baltic. A site was picked, and like God creating the world, on 1 June 1641 Kristiansand existed.

The town did not grow fast despite the king's decree, for it did not naturally and immediately attract trade away from the older

port of Arendal to the east, or from its own impoverished hinterland. Arendal by the mid-eighteenth century had become one of
Norway's principal ports, exporting timber and building those
beautiful sailing ships. The coming of steam killed the sailing ship
and hit Arendal hard. Despite the usual disastrous fires Kristiansand
survived, and the twentieth century has treated it kindly.

For many visitors it is the town from which they start their
Norwegian holiday: there is a direct sea connection with Harwich in
England, with Hirtshals in Denmark and with Amsterdam. Some
do not feel the need to travel much farther. Inland, the Setesdal is by
no means the sole attraction, and it only requires reasonable luck
with the weather to have a marvellous holiday on the coastline east
or west.

That was our good fortune. We found an empty camp site in
such an ideal position on a peninsula a few miles out that we spent
the whole of our last day there, sunbathing, swimming and exploring the rocks. We had earned a day without movement.

Yet there was so much in Norway that we had not seen, so much
that deserved a closer look. Any holiday in another country is no
more than a quick view through a door; a glimpse of another way of
life, a sampling of a different part of the earth's surface. A test of the
success of such a voyage is to ask whether one wants to return. We
did return, and hope to do so again.

Postscript

A nation is a complex entity. It is the physical land: the rock and earth, the lakes, rivers, forests and moors. It is the impress upon that land left by man, from ancient burial mounds to farms to the mountain-striding power transmission cables. It is the people who live on that land: both those of our time and all who have gone before. It is the culture of that people: their arts, their literature, their newspapers, their history, their myths about themselves and about the world around them.

This book is not an account of the Norwegian nation, and any reader who wants to know more about it will need to study some of the works listed in the bibliography. The emphasis has been on the land, for in Norway it is the land that dominates, and it is the land that most visitors come to see. Norway still has the feel of a pioneering nation; civilisation has not yet swamped the land; you can still think yourself to be the first person to gaze at a view, to discover a waterfall, to climb a mountainside. Norway reminds the traveller of the youth of the world, when men were closer to the earth and the earth was not hidden beneath swarms of men.

Norwegians themselves are passionate about the outdoor life. This was brought home to me again when I came across the statistics on violent deaths in Norway. In recent years deaths from falls have always outdistanced deaths from land transport and from drowning —the two next most frequent causes. Few children fall to their deaths. It is the adults who do so, and it must be that they keep falling off the mountains up which they rush at every opportunity. Where else in the western world does gravity kill more people than the motor car?

Despite Norway's vast areas of unproductive mountain and

moorland, the change in the material conditions of life during the last 100 years has been phenomenal. No account of travel in Norway in the nineteenth century that I have read is without its paragraphs on the dirt and the fleas, the discomfort of the cheaper country staging-posts, and the general backwardness and poverty of the nation. At that time it probably seemed impossible that such a country, with no coal, few known minerals, and so little cultivatable land, could ever be other than an exporter of timber and fish, a playground for rich anglers, and a dependency of its neighbours.

Nowadays few Europeans have a higher standard of living. From being a land in which the majority was engaged in making a poor living from fishing, farming and forestry, Norway has become a land where the majority is engaged in making a good living from industry and service occupations. Visitors will not, as a rule, see the obvious signs of industrialisation, as they can in Britain or Germany, for much of it is hidden at the heads of remote fjords, or inside mountains, or in those south-eastern parts where few explore, or on the high seas in ships which may never see the Norwegian coastline. The power-transmission lines are still the most visible signature of *norsk* industry.

The change can be illustrated by the story of emigration, a traumatic phase of Norwegian history. From 5 July 1825, when the first boatload of fifty-two Quakers sailed for New York, a broadening stream of emigrants left the country, mostly for the United States. The record year was 1882, when about 29,000 emigrated. By the 1920s well over three-quarters of a million people had gone, a massive exodus when compared with the total population (in 1801, about 883,000; it had increased to above 2 million by 1895). Now there is hardly a family in Norway that does not have American relatives.

Land shortage, poverty, debt, religious intolerance, lack of social and legal equality, dissatisfaction with a society which at that time restricted the vote to men with property and did little to relieve conditions for the small farmer and the labourer—these and other factors sent people to try their luck in America. For a century 'America fever' raged.

The American Immigration Act of 1924, followed by the Great Slump, cut off the flow of emigrants. At about the same time Norway itself was becoming a land of opportunity. The 1970 figures show that emigration only just outweighs immigration, that both are on a small scale, and that traffic to and from the United States is not of much significance (about 3,000 each way).

So Norway is no longer a country from which men are driven by poverty. Nowadays the human export trade is in trained experts— engineers, doctors, architects, technological specialists of all kinds— who spend a few years overseas and then return.

No one can be certain that Norway will sustain its present prosperity. The fortunes of all nations fluctuate, often for reasons beyond their control. Even more than Britain, Norway is sensitive to world conditions, for it depends heavily for food, for the raw materials that feed its industry, and for capital, on supplies from abroad. The expansion of hydro-electric power cannot continue indefinitely. Indeed it is predicted that the limit will be reached in 10–20 years. To offset this a mixture of oil-fired and nuclear generating plants are planned, and the recent discovery of North Sea oil must be a major encouragement (*plate 27*).

Modern Norway is a young nation, far younger than Denmark and Sweden, by whom it was in turn controlled. The flagpoles attached to each house, and the national flags that so often fly from them, are just one example of a continuing need to express unity and patriotism. Norwegians are perhaps still surprised by their own nationhood, and do not yet take it for granted.

Norway of course is part of Scandinavia, an area that has long been a geographical and a cultural whole, but never truly a political one. Man arrived late, following up the retreating ice sheet. And Scandinavia was not under Roman rule, with all that implies for good and bad. In this it is closer to Germany than to the rest of western Europe. Christianity came late to Scandinavia. Industrialisation came late, at least to Norway. Climate and the nature of the land have been hard taskmasters. These remarks are not made as criticisms. They are statements of fact to be kept in mind as one moves about the country and realises that Norwegian society is the product of a very different history from that of the French or British or Americans.

Present achievements are the more remarkable. The cost of living may be high (and is rising higher); Norwegians may grumble at the taxes and complain about their climate, yet it remains true for anyone to see that most of them live in considerable comfort, that they reap the benefits of an industrial society while avoiding the worst of its evils—slums, vast inequalities between the rich and the poor, a despoiled countryside. May it always be so.

APPENDIX

Practical Information

Roads

There is little need for concern about the roads of Norway. They are spectacular, they require care, but they are safe. Obviously a country of under 4 million people in an area considerably larger than the British Isles, with its 55 million—or nearly three times the size of Pennsylvania, USA, with a third of the population—will not have the kind of taxable income that permits asphalt on every track. An increasing mileage of main road is asphalted, and the surface on other roads is most often good. Minor roads that do not carry much traffic can provide a really smooth drive while tarmac can be deceptive, since here and there, for lack of a proper foundation, it can ambush the unwary with unexpected dips and waves.

Hairpin bends? In one morning you will learn to round them with cautious serenity. Apprehension is all in the mind.

Never drink and drive. Not only is the Norwegian law against this enforced and tough, but the roads require full concentration, for a mistake may land you not in a hedge or ditch, but in a lake or down a precipice.

Cars towing caravans will need ample power, and there are restrictions on the maximum size of the caravan.

Drive on the right of the road. There is an overall speed limit of 50 mph (80 kph) throughout the country. Norwegians keep to it and the police are strict. The only exception we met was on those few miles of motorway that leave Oslo for the south-west and the south-east. In towns the limit is 30 mph (50 kph).

Except on the gentler through routes, such as the E6 to the north, do not reckon to cover long distances. In a day, 150 miles plus some sightseeing is probably near the top limit for most people's stamina;

169

100 miles among the fjords would be a more sensible allowance. Anyway the country is so beautiful that it is criminal to be ambitious about distance. Ferries (see below) need a separate time calculation.

There are a good few tunnels, some short, some long, some lit, some unlit. The contrast between sunlight and darkness can be momentarily blinding, and dangerous. So slow down and switch on lights in good time.

Mountain passes should be open by early June, but in some years winter can hang on. They begin to snow up in October.

Petrol is available everywhere. It is a little cheaper near the large ports.

The Norwegian National Tourist Offices sell a useful booklet, *Motoring in Norway*, and give away a pamphlet, *Norway by Car*.

Ferries

A free annual timetable and fare list, *Car Ferry Services in Norway*, published in the spring, is also obtainable from the Norwegian National Tourist Offices. This covers the major ferry crossings. Since 1945, especially in the north, a number of the shorter water crossings have been bridged, so that older guide and travel books are not reliable in this respect. But there are scores of ferry crossings left, and a great pleasure they can be, providing a break for the driver, a chance for all to clean up in the washrooms, to eat and drink in the saloon, and always wonderful scenery.

North of Trondheim and among the islands of the west coast the ferries are not bookable in advance. Over the rest of the country most can be booked, though we never bothered. With one exception, the longest wait we had was fifteen minutes. However if you are tied to hotel reservations or a rendezvous with friends, it may be best to telephone ahead the day before.

Boarding and disembarking from ferries is done quickly, with no fuss. In fact crossing a mile or two of water in Norway is easier, safer, and probably quicker than crossing a medium-sized town in other lands. Ferries are not expensive.

Accommodation

As motorcaravanners we are not experts on this. There seem to be
hotels everywhere. There are about 180 youth hostels (open to
motorists), also pensions, chalets and huts (*hytter*), innumerable
rooms to let and over 1,000 camp sites, many with camping huts
(at which you supply your own bedding and catering equipment).

In towns and along the south coast the listed camping sites may
become full up. Some of them are open only from mid-June to near
the end of August, when the Norwegian schools restart, but we
found many open in early September. The smaller camp sites may
lack hot water and showers, but they are less crowded, quieter and
cleaner.

Norway is about 95 per cent more or less uninhabited forest and
mountain plateau. While much of this is inaccessible to cars, there is
still a wide choice of side road and track along which to search for a
camping space of your own. If the land is obviously private, obtain
permission to camp. Do not light open fires in forest country.

Hotels in towns and in favoured fishing and walking centres also
tend to fill up. Visitors are advised to book ahead or arrive early.

Lists of chalets for hire, of hotels and of the better camp sites are
available from the Norwegian National Tourist Offices. Town
information centres can advise about most of these in their own
localities. In Oslo the railway's East Station has an accommodation
bureau that arranges the booking of rooms in private houses while
you wait.

Washrooms

The standard of cleanliness is high; the average public cloakroom is
a more presentable place than in, for example, France or Britain.
You can expect to find lavatories in railway stations, on ferries, at
the larger garages, in large supermarkets, attached to most cafés and
restaurants of any size, and in all hotels and camp sites. Camp-site
lavatories can be dirty, presumably because we foreigners do not all
have the Scandinavian zest for cleanliness. Some churches have

lavatories, especially in isolated country areas where the congrega-tion has had to travel some distance. These may be of the earth type in a wooden hut discreetly at the fringe of the churchyard.

Often washrooms are free; sometimes a coin through a slot opens the door. The same stairway down or up can lead to a subdivision inside for the two sexes. The signs for lavatories are varied: a cock and a hen, the usual male and female silhouettes, a red heart (both sexes, and bad luck to the slower). In words one finds: for women, *kvinner, kvinnor, dame*; and for men, *menn, herrer*. A general heading is *toalett* or *vaskerom*.

Language

It is obviously useful to speak Norwegian, but not essential. Our experience was that in towns a fair proportion of adults know some English, while in the country the proportion is less and young people are the best bet. By the late 1950s all urban communities and about 30 per cent of the rural districts had introduced English into normal schools; by 1969 the teaching of English was universal. Thus most teenagers should know enough English to tell you the way, or the weather forecast, or where to buy milk or a new pair of sunglasses.

Spoken Norwegian makes no sense whatever to an English-speaking foreigner, though it sounds beautiful. The written language is often comprehensible. This is partly because many English words derive from the time when Danes and Norwegians settled large areas of eastern and northern England, and partly because modern Norwegian has absorbed in reverse a number of English words in a recognisable form.

There is unfortunately a built-in disincentive to learning Nor-wegian—there are at least three languages. There is *riksmål* or *bokmål*, a kind of Danish-based Norwegian that evolved in the south-east; there is *landsmål* or *nynorsk*, a synthetic language standardised in the mid-nineteenth century and based on the medieval country dialects of the western districts; and there is *samnnorsk*, an artificial blend of the two, put forward in 1938. There have also been several spelling reforms in this century alone. Norwegians themselves get confused. If you do learn Norwegian, you will also be understood nearly everywhere in Denmark and Sweden.

Bibliography

The books listed below are those which I have found useful and interesting. They include every book cited in the text. There is a considerable literature in English on Norway, though much of it is out of print. I have not read the whole of that literature (especially books in English published in Norway) and I do not list all that I have looked at. The Norwegian National Tourist Offices usually stock a number of useful booklets, some free, the rest not costly. I list a few of these below.

ABRAHAMSEN, Helge. *Building in Norway: An Architectural Outline* (Royal Norwegian Ministry of Foreign Affairs, 1959)

ANDERSSON, Aron. *The Art of Scandinavia*, vol 2 (Paul Hamlyn, 1970; original French ed, 1969). For vol 1, see ANKER

ANKER, Peter. *The Art of Scandinavia*, vol 1 (Paul Hamlyn, 1970; original French ed, 1969). This volume contains a long section, with many illustrations, on stave churches. For vol 2, see ANDERSSON

ASH, Bernard. *Norway 1940* (Cassell, 1964). A somewhat emotional account of the British part in the Norwegian campaign, with plenty of quotations from participants. MOULTON to be preferred

BAEDEKER. *Scandinavia* (1963 ed)

BRØNDSTED, Johannes. *The Vikings* (Penguin, revised trans, 1965)

CARAMAN, Philip. *Norway* (Longmans, 1969). A well-written and intelligent account by a Catholic priest, based upon personal journeys

CONNERY, Donald. *The Scandinavians* (Eyre & Spottiswoode, 1966). A reporter's account, and a very good one, perhaps the best, of post-war Scandinavia

DAVIDSON, Hilda. *Pagan Scandinavia*, 'Ancient Peoples and Places' series (Thams & Hudson, 1967). The two Davidsons here listed are in fact one

DAVIDSON, H. R. Ellis. *Gods and Myths of Northern Europe* (Penguin, 1964)

DERRY, T. K. *The Campaign in Norway* (HMSO, 1952). The official war history

DERRY, T. K. *A Short History of Norway* (Allen & Unwin, 2nd ed, 1968)
A standard one-volume history

DOUGLAS, John. *The Arctic Highway: A Road and Its Setting* (David & Charles, 1972). Certainly a book to possess if exploring Norway north of Mo i Rana

DU CHAILLU, Paul B. *The Land of the Midnight Sun: Summer and Winter journeys through Sweden, Norway, Lapland and Northern Finland* (George Newnes, new ed, 1899). The journeys were undertaken between 1871 and 1878

Facts About Norway ('Aftenposten', Oslo, 13th ed, 1972). A compact paperback available from the Norwegian National Tourist Offices

GJAEREVOLL, Olav and JØRGENSEN, Reidar. *Mountain Flowers of Scandinavia* (Trondheim, 3rd ed, 1972). A pocket flora covering some 150 species. It is the fate of all such selections never to contain the flowers one meets

HAGEN, Anders. *Norway*, 'Ancient Peoples and Places' series. (Thames & Hudson, 1967). Unsatisfactory, but the only book available on prehistoric Norway

HAY, Doddy. *Your Guide to Norway* (Alvin Redman, 1968)

HODIN, J. P. *Edvard Munch* (Thames & Hudson, 1972). A standard work, and available in paperback

Hrafnkel's Saga and Other Stories, trans with an introduction by Hermann Pálsson. (Penguin, 1971)

JONES, Gwyn. *A History of the Vikings* (Oxford University Press, 1968). A fine and comprehensive account

KNUDSON, Ole. *Norway at Work: A Survey of the Principal Branches of the Economy* (Johan Grundt Tanum Forlag, Oslo, 1972). A useful brief account. One of a series of short paperbacks on many aspects of Norwegian life in the 'Tokens of Norway' series, to be found in most Norwegian bookshops

METCALFE, Rev Frederick. *The Oxonian in Norway: Notes of Excursions in That Country in 1854-1855*, 2 vols (Hurst & Blackett, 1856)

MILLWARD, Roy. *Scandinavian Lands* (Macmillan, 1964). There are more recent geographies, and in some respects this is out of date. But it is a pleasure to read

Mini-Facts about Norway 1972. (The Royal Ministry of Foreign Affairs, Oslo, 1973)

MOULTON, J. L. *The Norwegian Campaign of 1940: A Study of Warfare in Three Dimensions* (Eyre & Spottiswoode, 1966). A very professional account by a soldier of the actions of all combatants

Njal's Saga, trans with an introduction by Magnus Magnusson and Hermann Pálsson (Penguin, 1960)

ØVSTEDAL, Barbara. *Norway* (Batsford, 1973)

PAULSSON, T. *Scandinavian Architecture: Buildings and Society in Denmark, Finland, Norway, and Sweden from the Iron Age until Today* (Leonard Hill, 1958). Good at giving the historical situations that have led to each period and type of building

POPPERWELL, Ronald G. *Norway*, 'Nations of the Modern World' series (Benn, 1972). The best single volume on Norway that I have read. Concerned mostly with the history and culture of the nineteenth and twentieth centuries

SIMPSON, Jacqueline. *Everyday Life in the Viking Age* (Batsford, 1967; Carousel paperback, 1971). Authoritative, readable

SOMME, Axel (ed). *A Geography of Norden* (Heinemann, 3rd ed, 1968). A basic book for an understanding of the area. The contributors are Scandinavian

STAGG, Frank Noel. *South Norway* (Allen & Unwin, 1958). Discursive, disjointed, but full of fascinating historical information. Crippled by the absence of good maps; those supplied are a joke. Commander Stagg has also written (1952–9): *North Norway, The Heart of Norway, West Norway and Its Fjords, East Norway and Its Frontier*

STURLUSON, Snorri. *Heimskringla: The Olaf Sagas, Sagas of the Norse Kings*, trans Samuel Laing; revised and introduced by Jacqueline Simpson and Peter Foote (Dent, Everyman's Library, vols 717, 847, 1961 and 1964). Available in paperback. The greatest of the Icelandic Sagas containing accounts of many early Norwegian kings

Vinland Sagas: The Norse Discovery of America, trans with an introduction by Magnus Magnusson and Hermann Pálsson (Penguin, 1965)

VORREN, Ørnulv (ed). *Norway North of 65* (Oslo University Press, 1960; Allen & Unwin, 1961). Chapters by various experts. For the visitor to Norway north of 65° latitude

WELLE-STRAND, Erling. *Tourist in Norway* ('Aftenposten', Oslo, 4th ed, 1971). A useful paperback guide usually available from the Norwegian National Tourist Offices

WELLE-STRAND, Erling and PRAG, Per. *Motoring in Norway* (Norway Travel Association, 1972). A paperback guide arranged by routes; usually available from the Norwegian National Tourist Offices

WILLIAMS, W. Mattieu. *Through Norway with a Knapsack* (Smith, Elder &

Co, 1859). An amusing account of a solo walk through Norway. The same author wrote *Through Norway with Ladies* (1877), which I have not read

WILSON, David. *The Vikings and Their Origins: Scandinavia in the First Millennium* (Thames & Hudson, 1970). A good, beautifully illustrated short introduction, also available in paper back.

Maps

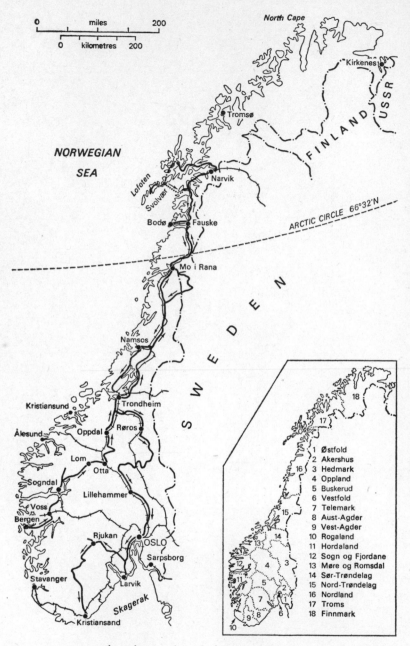

1   *Norway complete, showing the author's journey with (inset) a map outlining the counties*

Map labels:

North Cape
Kirkenes
Tromsø
NORWEGIAN SEA
Lofoten
Svolvær
Narvik
FINLAND
USSR
ARCTIC CIRCLE 66°32'N
Bodø   Fauske
Mo i Rana
SWEDEN
Namsos
Kristiansund
Trondheim
Ålesund   Oppdal   Røros
Lom
Otta
Sogndal   Lillehammer
Voss
Bergen
Rjukan   OSLO
Sarpsborg
Stavanger   Larvik
Skagerak
Kristiansand

miles   200
kilometres   200

Inset legend:

1 Østfold
2 Akershus
3 Hedmark
4 Oppland
5 Buskerud
6 Vestfold
7 Telemark
8 Aust-Agder
9 Vest-Agder
10 Rogaland
11 Hordaland
12 Sogn og Fjordane
13 Møre og Romsdal
14 Sør-Trøndelag
15 Nord-Trøndelag
16 Nordland
17 Troms
18 Finnmark

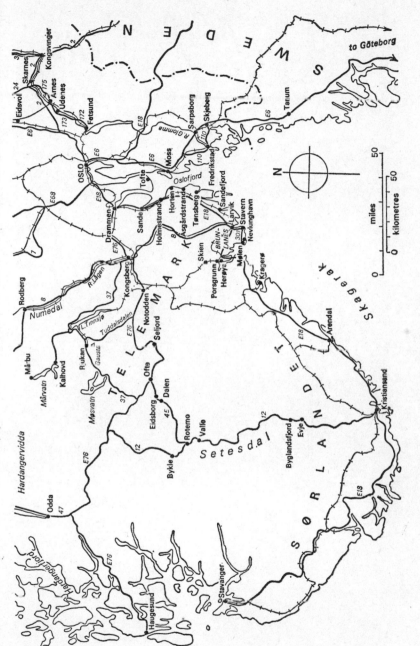

2   Southern Norway

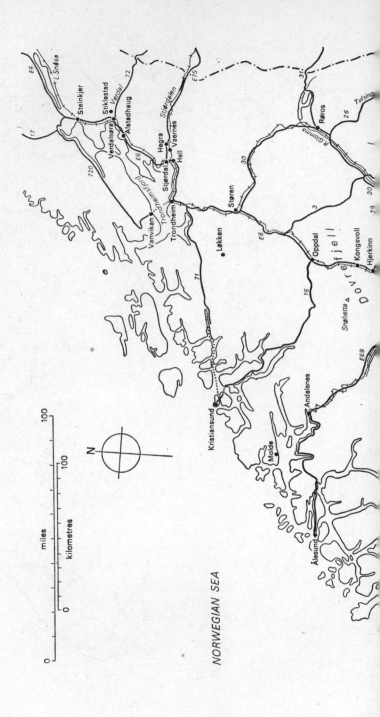

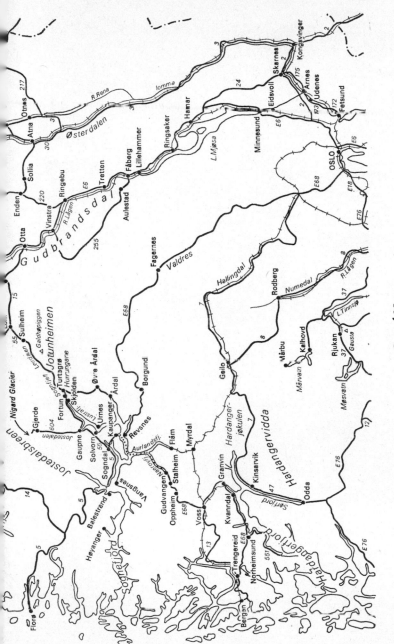

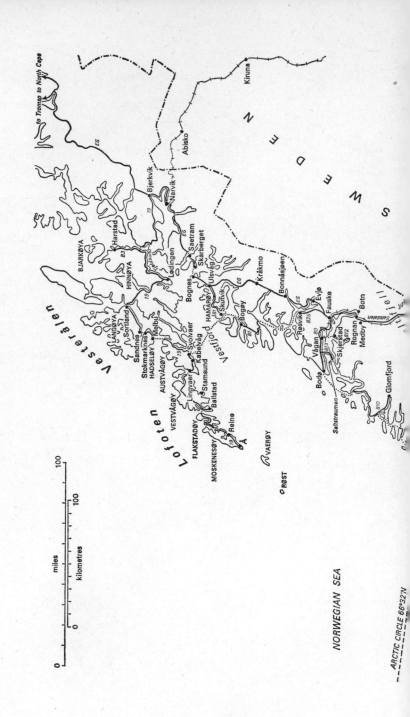

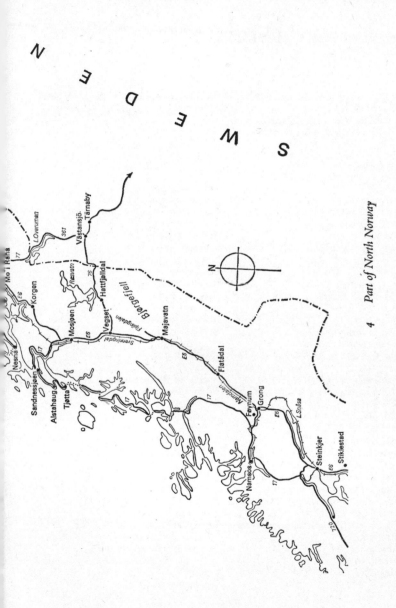

4 *Part of North Norway*

Index

Note: In Norwegian the letters æ, ø and å come at the end of the alphabet. However, in this index they are placed where the English-speaking reader will be more likely to look for them.

Numbers in *italic* refer to plates.

190   INDEX

Oslofjorden, 119, 136, 141, 149, 150
Østerdalen, 122-3, 127, 150
Østerdalsisen glacier, 106, 109
Østfold, 134, 149
Otnes, 122
Otta, 51
Øveruman, Lake, 110
Øvre Årdal, 38, 47
Øvre Rendal, 122
Øyeren, Lake, 136

Painting, see Arts
Peer Gynt, 127
Peer Gynt road, 127
Polar Circle, see Arctic Circle
Population, 12, 20, 169; of Oslo, 150
Power stations, see Hydro-electric
    power
Prehistoric Norway, 23, 65, 67-9,
    114, 134, 142, 149, 158; see also
    Burial mounds, Rock carvings
Pyrites, see Mining

Rådhuset, Oslo, 108, 125, 146
Railways (general), 150; see also
    Communications
Rana fjord, 105, 109
Rasmus Meyer Collection, Bergen,
    20-1
Reindeer, 121n, 144, 158
Reinforshei, salmon ladder at, 74-5
Religion: beginnings of Christianity,
    42, 58-9, 167; the Lutheran
    Reformation, 16, 41, 59; pre-
    Christian, 142; see also Churches,
    Stave churches
Rena valley, 122
Revsnes, 34
Ringebu, 124, 127
Ringebu stave church, 42, 124
Ringsaker, St Olaf's church, 133, 151
Ringve Museum of Musical History,
    Trondheim, 63-4
Rjukan, 39, 158-60
Roads (general), 25, 82-3, 169-70;
    see also Arctic Highway, Routes
Rock carvings, 67-9, 70, 80, 83, 86,
    132, 134, 144; see also Burial
    mounds, Prehistoric Norway
Rognan, 76
Rombaksbotn, 85, 87

Rondane mountains, 51, 123-4, 127
Røros, 118, 119-21, 156; church, 89,
    120
Røssvoll, 106
Røst (bird islands), 78
Røsvatn, Lake, 112
Røsvik, 81, 103
Rotemo, 162, 163
Routes: 2: 133; 3: 122; E6: 27, 51,
    55, 56, 69, 70, 73, 75, 81, 83, 106,
    110, 112, 114, 118, 127, 133, 136,
    169, see also Arctic Highways; 7:
    29, 158; 8: 156, 157; 13: 29n; 15:
    27; 17: 114, 116; 19: 83, 87, 88, 91,
    93; 24: 133; 26: 121; 27: 123; 30:
    118; 31: 121; 37: 157, 158; 45: 162;
    55: 27, 40, 44, 47, 49; E68: 25, 27,
    31; E75: 67; 76: 110, 112; E76:
    162; 77: 110; 80: 77, 78; 81: 83,
    103; 83: 91; 110: 134; 172: 136;
    173: 134, 136; 175: 133; 217: 121;
    220: 123; 301: 154; 361: 112
    (Sweden); 551: 25, 26; 604: 44;
    720: 116; 760: 113; 805: 78, 105,
    114 (the Blue Road); 810: 78;
    812: 78; 813: 77; 815: 99; 826: 103

Saetran, 84
Sagas, Icelandic, 11, 19
Sagfjord, 83
Saltdalen, 76, 78
Saltdalsfjord, 76
Saltfjell, 75
Saltfjord, 77
Saltstraumen maelstrom, 77-8
Samivrkelag cooperative shops, 120
Sandnes, 93
Sandvig, Anders, 128, 129
Sandvig Collection, Lillehammer,
    128-32
Sarpsborg, 134
Scandinavia, 37, 99, 111-12, 136-7,
    167
Scotland, 12, 15, 28, 141
Sculpture, see Arts
Sealing/seals, 34, 99
Seattle, 21
Seljord church, 89, 162
Seter, 31, 131-2
Setesdalen, 162-3
Ship burials, 142